Where In The WORLD?
United States and Capitals, Plus Physical Features!

Created by Amanda Predmore

STUDENT WORKBOOK

COMPANION BOOK:
Teaching & Student Resource Book with Historical Tid-Bits and Master Maps can be found for purchase at http://bit.ly/WITWgeo

A Classically Based Geography Curriculum On
UNITED STATES AND CAPITALS and US PHYSICAL FEATURES
with HISTORICAL, CULTURAL, SCIENTIFIC, & ENVIRONMENTAL TID-BITS

Part of the **Where in the World** Geography Series
Where the student's learn to memorize through drawing and discussion.
http://bit.ly/WhereInTheWorldGeo

All the Parts Get to Know the Curriculum!

BOOK 1

Book 1 is the Teaching Resource Guide. This guide includes Parts 1, 2, & 3 for each lesson.

BOOK 2

Book 2 is the Worksheet Book. This book includes Parts 4 & 5 for each lesson.

There are 2 books that work as a team! These two books, together, have 5 parts for each lesson. Take a look below to understand each part and where they can be found!

Parts of each lesson

1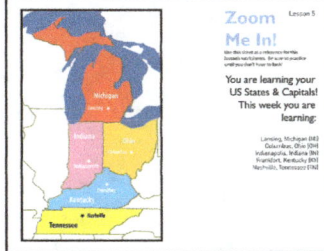

Closer Look! A map showing new geography being learned, alongside geography learned over the last 6 lessons! This map is located in the Teaching Resource Guide (Book 1) to be used as a reference when doing review work.

2

Zoom me in! A map zoomed in to show just the new geography being learned. This map reflects the worksheet called "Now, let's trace, shade, & label!" This map is a great reference when first learning the geography. This map is located in the Teaching Resource Guide (Book 1) to be used as a reference as needed.

3

Tid-Bits! This is the place where you find all of the tid-bits of history, culture, geographical information, science, animals, and more, relating directly to the geography being learned! This section is located in the Teaching Resource Guide (Book 1).

4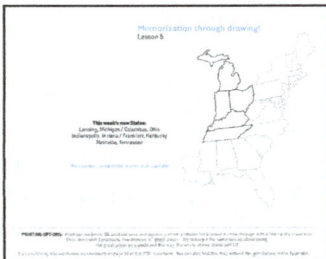

Worksheet - 1 per lesson: "Now, let's trace, shade, & label!" This worksheet is the first introduction to the geography being learned! A gentle way to become familiar with the geography while learning about these places through the tid-bits of information available in the teaching resource guide. This section is located within the Worksheet Book (Book 2).

5

Worksheets - 2 per lesson: "Memorization Through Repetition" This worksheet includes the new geography PLUS geography for the last 6 lessons. A gentle way to memorize. Before you know it, the "Closer Look!" map won't be needed! This section is located within the Worksheet Book (Book 2).

TIPS FOR BEING PREPARED!

Having the right tools makes a difference in the quality of drawing and labeling. It is recommend that tracing and coloring be done with colored pencils.

In addition, a fine point sharpie works well over the colored pencil, it is suggested to have a blue for rivers, a black for geography labeling and red for cities. Most geography is the same grouping of colors. Pre-grouping the needed colored pencils and pens into a geo-kit will be helpful.

**Recommended Product:
Sharpie Pen Stylo Fine Point**

Copyright © 2020 by Amanda Predmore

Where in the World?
United States and Capitals, plus Physical Features!

STUDENT WORKBOOK

Memorize and Engage Geography Through
Repetition and Discussion

http://bit.ly/WhereInTheWorldGeo

All rights reserved. See restrictions and allowances below.

This book or any portion thereof may not be reproduced and is licensed by purchase for the use of educational material for one homeschool family, or one student in a classroom. Copy of worksheets for personal use in your family is permitted. Beyond this you may not transmit or distribute without express written permission of the author/designer except for brief quotations in a book review.

ISBN 978-1-7325085-3-8

Printed in the United States of America

TABLE OF Contents

All the Parts - Get to Know the Curriculum ii

Introductory Lesson Worksheets (Part 4) - "Now, Let's Trace, Shade, & Label!

Lesson 1 1	Lesson 7 13	Lesson 13 25	Lesson 19 37
Lesson 2 3	Lesson 8 15	Lesson 14 27	Lesson 20 39
Lesson 3 5	Lesson 9 17	Lesson 15 29	Lesson 21 41
Lesson 4 7	Lesson 10 19	Lesson 16 31	Lesson 22 43
Lesson 5 9	Lesson 11 21	Lesson 17 33	Lesson 23 45
Lesson 6 11	Lesson 12 23	Lesson 18 35	Lesson 24 47

TrueReview - Memorization Through Repetition Lesson Worksheets (Part 5)

TrueReview Schedule 50

Lesson 1 51	Lesson 7 63	Lesson 13 75	Lesson 19 87
Lesson 2 53	Lesson 8 65	Lesson 14 77	Lesson 20 89
Lesson 3 55	Lesson 9 67	Lesson 15 79	Lesson 21 91
Lesson 4 57	Lesson 10 69	Lesson 16 81	Lesson 22 93
Lesson 5 59	Lesson 11 71	Lesson 17 83	Lesson 23 95
Lesson 6 61	Lesson 12 73	Lesson 18 85	Lesson 24 97

Teaching Aids - Pull out maps for posting & copying 111
Along the Way Progression Chart 119
Certificate of Completion 121

Now, let's trace, draw, and label!
An introductory worksheet for each lesson.

Lesson 1

Now, let's trace, shade, & label!

✓	Label these U.S. States & Capitals	Trace & Shade in These Colors
	Augusta, Maine	(light blue)
	Concord, New Hampshire	(pink)
	Boston, Massachusetts	(yellow)
	Providence, Rhode Island	(purple)
	Hartford, Connecticut	(green)

Optional Cut & Paste Labels:

| Augusta, Maine | Concord, New Hampshire | Boston, Massachusetts | Providence, Rhode Island | Hartford, Connecticut |

Lesson 2

Now, let's trace, shade, & label!

	U.S. States & Capitals	Trace & Shade in These Colors
✓	Montpelier, Vermont	(light blue)
	Albany, New York	(orange)
	Trenton, New Jersey	(yellow)
	Harrisburg, Pennsylvania	(green)
	Dover, Delaware	(purple)
	Be sure to label the capital next to the star!	☆

Optional Cut & Paste Labels: ✂

| Montpelier, Vermont | Albany, New York | Trenton, New Jersey | Harrisburg, Pennsylvania | Dover, Delaware |

Lesson 3

Now, let's trace, shade, & label!

	U.S. States & Capitals	Trace & Color in These Colors
	Annapolis, Maryland	
	Richmond, Virginia	
	Charleston, West Virginia	
	Raleigh, North Carolina	
	Columbia, South Carolina	
	Washington D.C.	★

Be sure to label the capital next to the star! ☆

Optional Cut & Paste Labels:

- ✂

| Annapolis, Maryland | Richmond, Virginia | Charleston, West Virginia | Raleigh, North Carolina | Columbia, South Carolina |

Lesson 4

Now, let's trace, shade, & label!

✓	U.S. States & Capitals	Trace & Color in These Colors
	Atlanta, Georgia	🟦
	Tallahassee, Florida	🟧
	Montgomery, Alabama	🟩
	Jackson, Mississippi	🟪
	Baton Rouge, Louisiana	🟨
	Be sure to label the capital next to the star!	☆

Optional Cut & Paste Labels:

- -

| Atlanta, Georgia | Tallahassee, Florida | Montgomery, Alabama | Jackson, Mississippi | Baton Rouge, Louisiana |

Lesson 5

Now, let's trace, shade, & label!

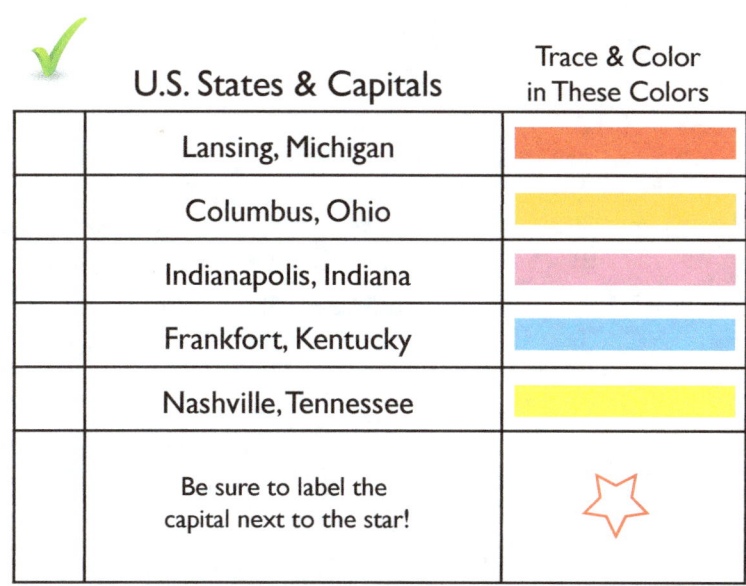

	U.S. States & Capitals	Trace & Color in These Colors
	Lansing, Michigan	🟧
	Columbus, Ohio	🟨
	Indianapolis, Indiana	🟪
	Frankfort, Kentucky	🟦
	Nashville, Tennessee	🟨
	Be sure to label the capital next to the star!	☆

Optional Cut & Paste Labels

Lansing, Michigan | Columbus, Ohio

Indianapolis, Indiana | Frankfort, Kentucky

Nashville, Tennessee

Now, let's trace, shade, & label!

Lesson 6

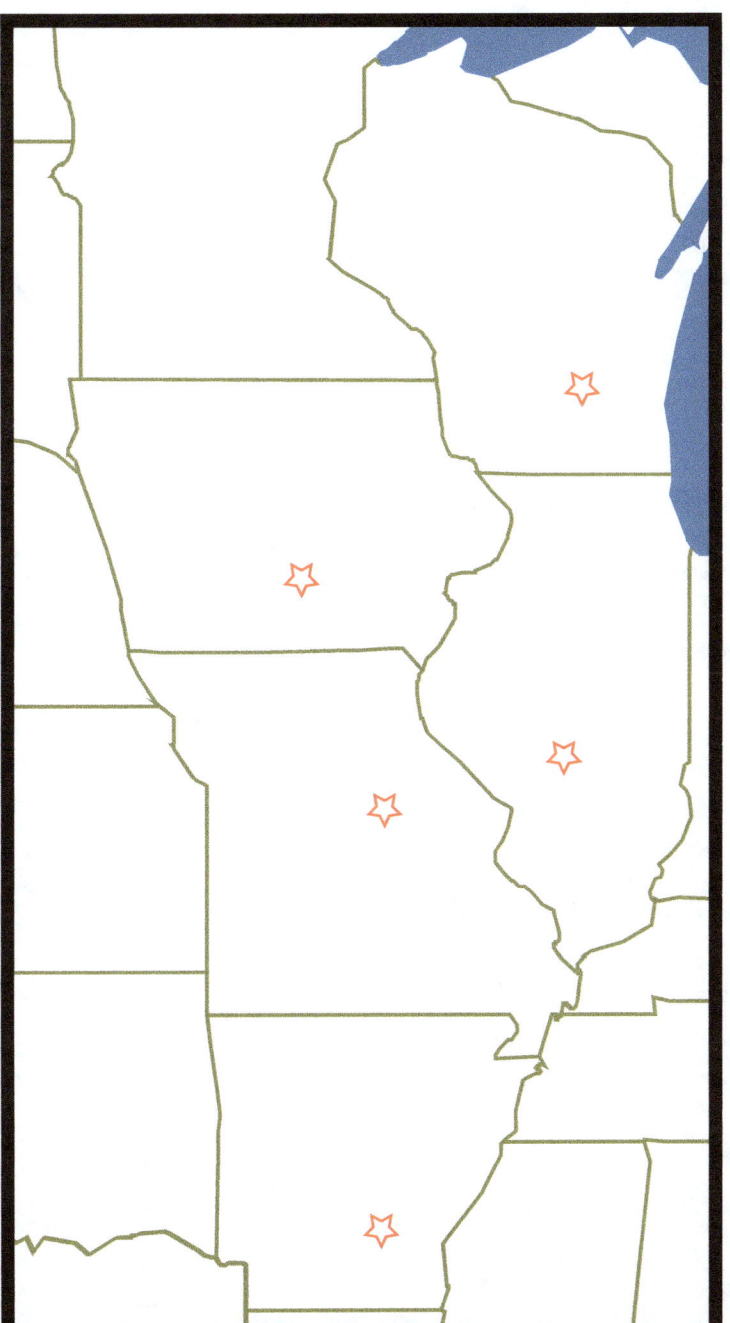

	U.S. States & Capitals	Trace & shade in these colors
✓	Madison, Wisconsin	🟨
	Springfield, Illinois	🟪
	Des Moines, Iowa	🟦
	Jefferson City, Missouri	🟪
	Little Rock, Arkansas	🟧
	Be sure to label the capital next to the star! If you are using the labels below, you can cut the label in half if needed.	☆

Optional Cut & Paste Labels

| Madison, Wisconsin | Springfield, Illinois | Des Moines, Iowa |

| Jefferson City, Missouri | Little Rock, Arkansas |

11

Lesson 7

Now, let's trace, shade, & label!

	U.S. States & Capitals	Trace & shade in these colors
✓	St. Paul, Minnesota	🟧
	Bismarck, North Dakota	🟦
	Pierre, South Dakota	🟨
	Cheyenne, Wyoming	🟪
	Lincoln, Nebraska	🟪
	Be sure to label the capital next to the star! If you are using the labels below, you can cut the label in half if needed.	☆

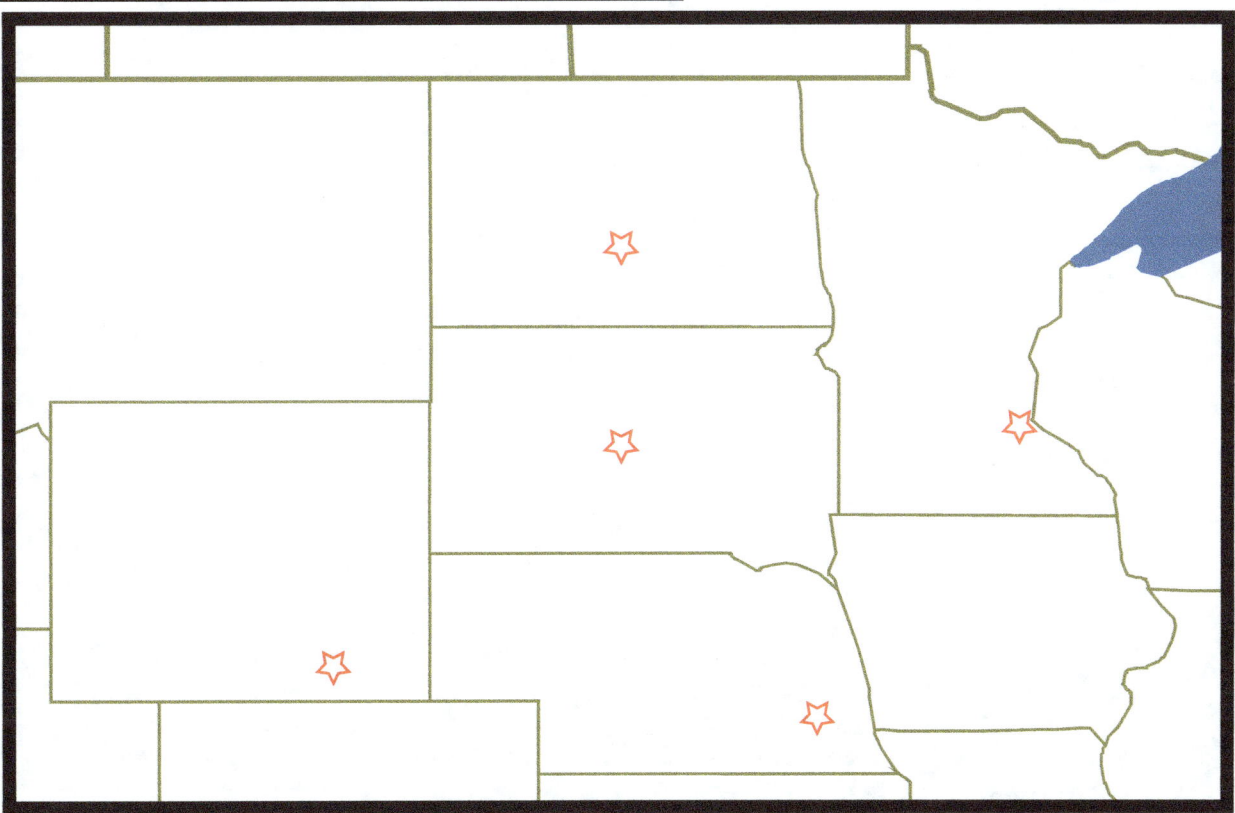

Optional Cut & Paste Labels

- St. Paul Minnesota
- Bismarck, North Dakota
- Pierre, South Dakota
- Cheyenne, Wyoming
- Lincoln, Nebraska

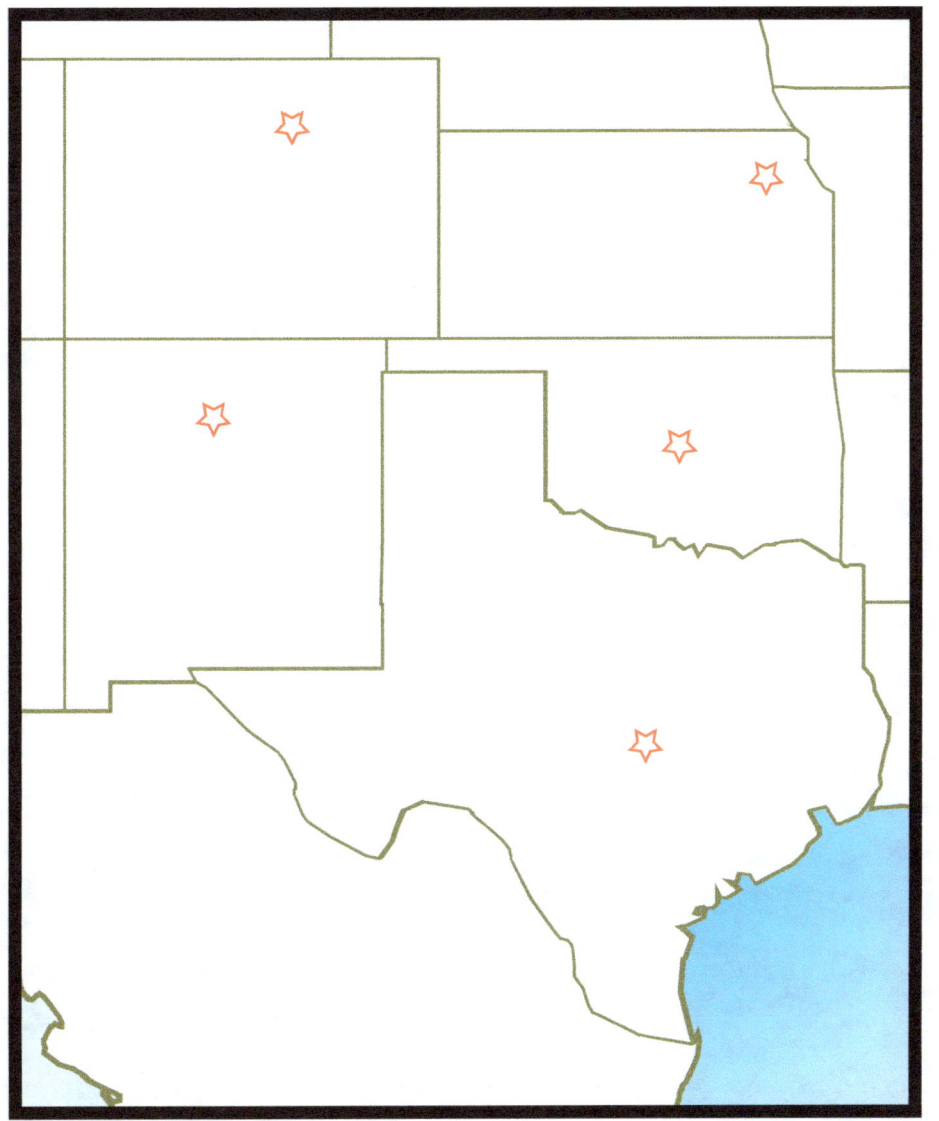

Now, let's trace, shade, & label!

Lesson 8

✓ U.S. States & Capitals | Trace & shade in these colors

	U.S. States & Capitals	
	Topeka, Kansas	🟦
	Oklahoma City, Oklahoma	🟨
	Austin, Texas	🟪
	Denver, Colorado	🟩
	Santa Fe, New Mexico	🟥
	Be sure to label the capital next to the star! If you are using the labels below, you can cut the label in half if needed.	☆

Optional Cut & Paste Labels

- -

| Topeka, Kansas | Oklahoma City, Oklahoma | Austin, Texas | Denver, Colorado | Santa Fe, New Mexico |

Now, let's trace, shade, & label!

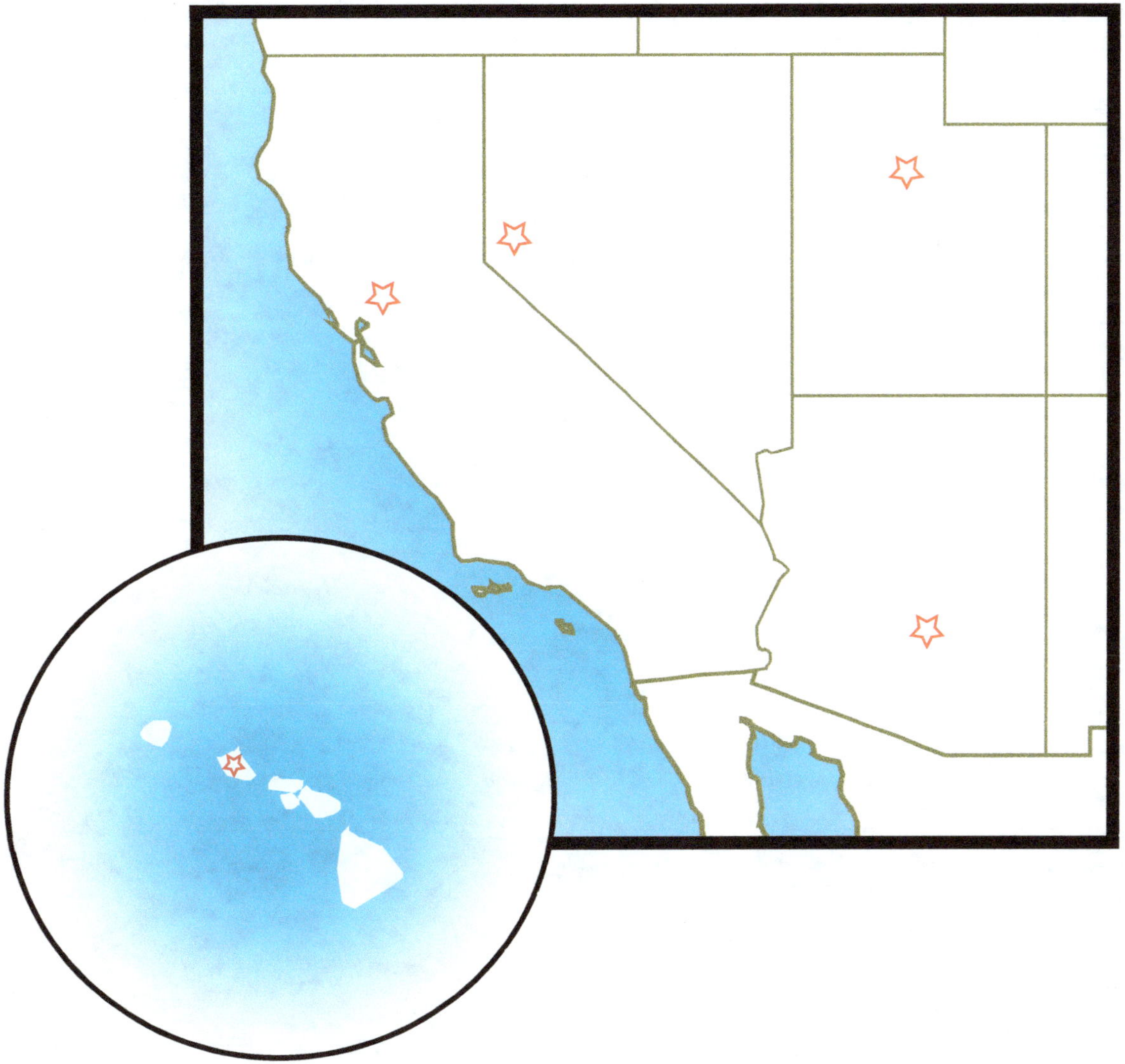

Lesson 9

✓	U.S. States & Capitals	Trace & shade in these colors
	Salt Lake City, Utah	🟪
	Phoenix, Arizona	🟨
	Carson City, Nevada	🟦
	Sacramento, California	🟧
	Honolulu, Hawaii	🟩
	Be sure to label the capital next to the star! *If you are using the labels below, you can cut the label in half if needed.*	☆

Optional Cut & Paste Labels

| Salt Lake City, Utah | Phoenix, Arizona | Carson City, Nevada | Sacramento, California | Honolulu, Hawaii |

17

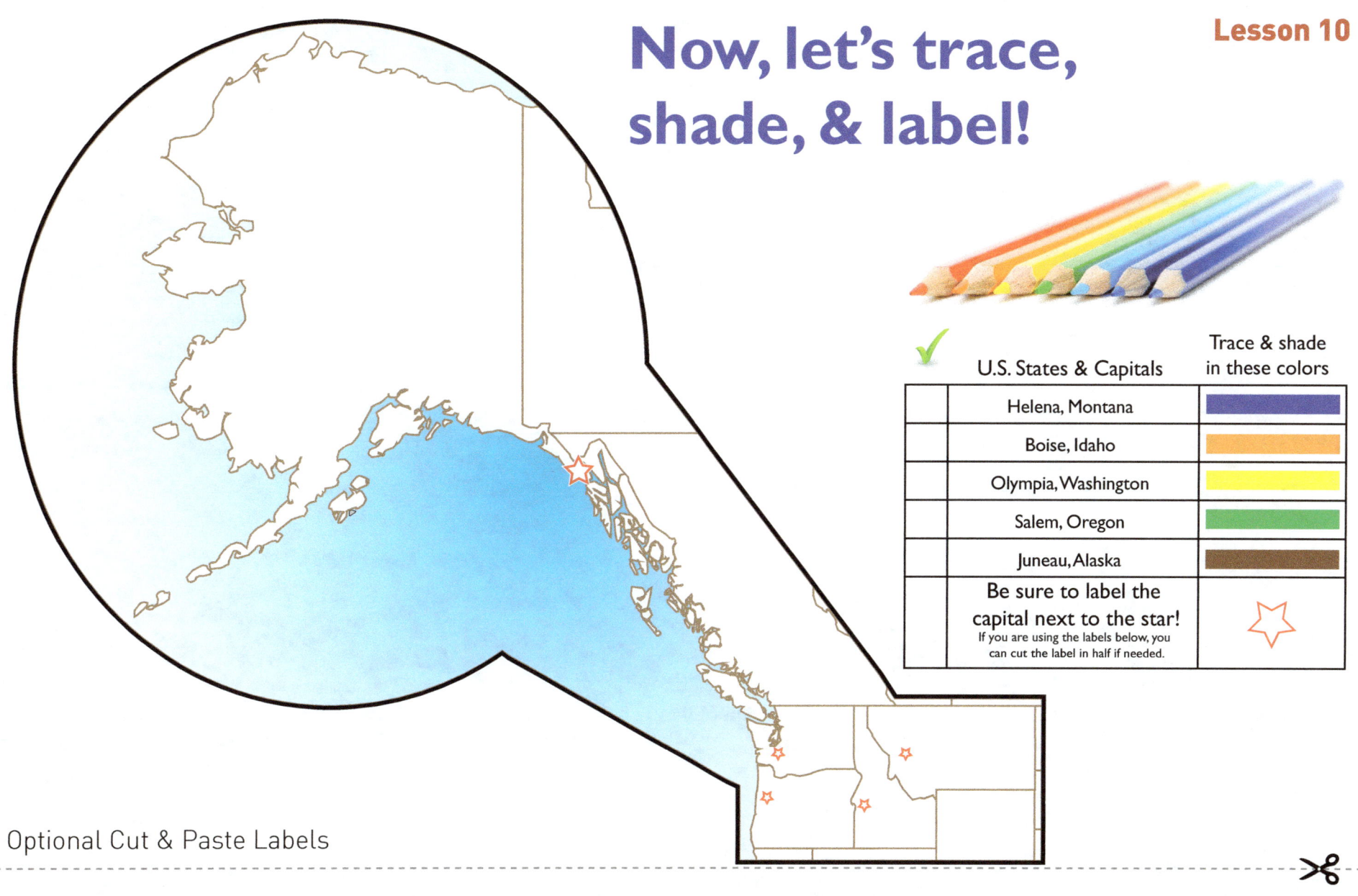

Lesson 11

Now, let's trace, shade, & label!

	Geography to Shade & Label	Trace/Draw in these colors and/or shapes
	White Mountains	🟫
	Green Mountains	🟩
	Adirondack Mountains	🟦
	Allegheny Mountains	🟨

No triangles are needed to represent the mountains.

White Mountains | Green Mountains | Adirondack Mountains | Allegheny Mountains

Optional Cut & Paste Labels

Now, let's trace, shade, & label!

Lesson 12

✓ **GEOGRAPHY TO SHADE & LABEL**

Shade in these different Mountains, The Great Valley and label Mt. Mitchell

	The Great Valley	🟩
	The Blue Ridge Mountains	🟦
	The Great Smoky Mountains	🟪
	Cumberland Mountains	🟥
	Mt. Mitchell	▲

Shading the areas where the mountains are without drawing triangles is sufficient.

Optional Cut & Paste Labels

- ✂ - - - -

| The Great Valley | Blue Ridge Mountains | Great Smoky Mountains | Cumberland Mountains | Mt. Mitchell |

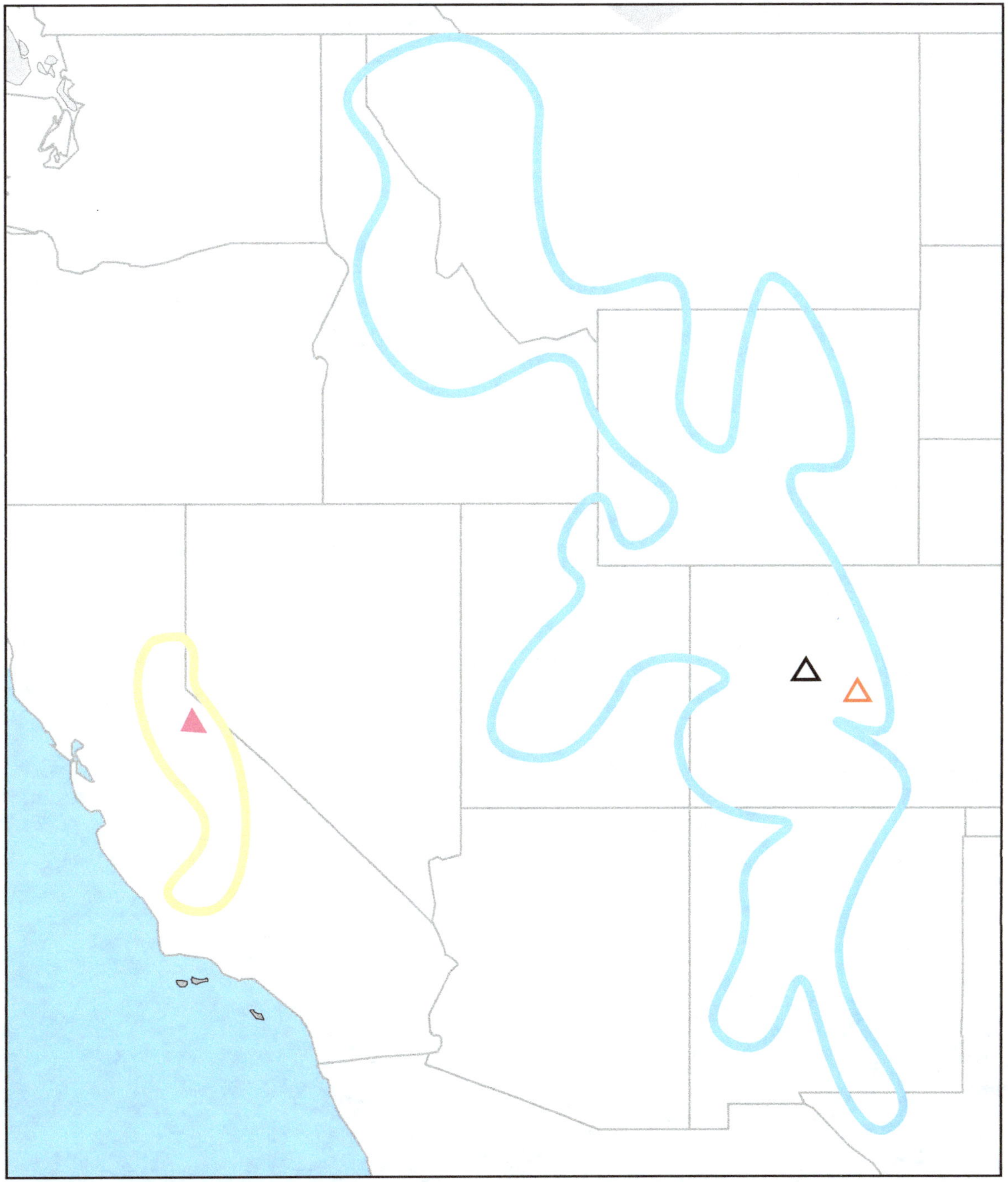

Now, let's trace, shade, & label!

Lesson 13

✓ **GEOGRAPHY TO SHADE & LABEL**

Shade in these colors. Label the individual mountains.

Geography	Color/Symbol
Rocky Mountains	light blue
Pikes Peak	orange △
Mt. Elbert	black △
Sierra Nevada Mountains	yellow
Mt. Whitney	pink ▲

Shading the areas where mountain ranges are without drawing triangles is sufficient.

Optional Cut & Paste Labels

| Rocky Mountains | Pikes Peak |

| Mt. Elbert | Sierra Nevadas |

| Mt. Whitney |

25

Now, let's trace, shade, & label!

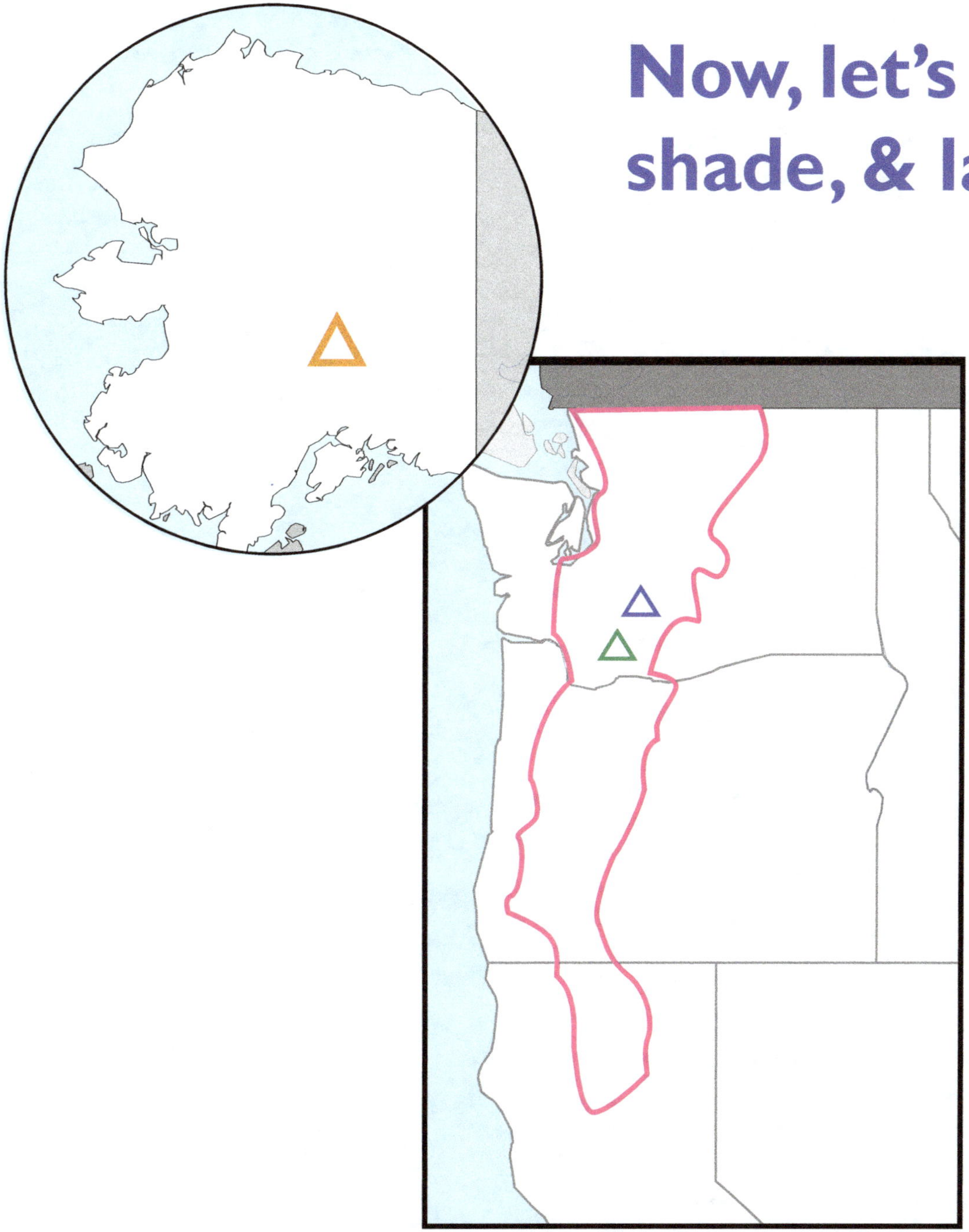

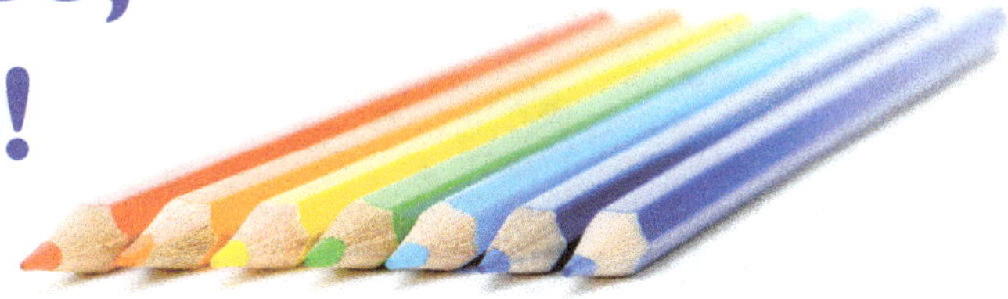

Lesson 14

✓	GEOGRAPHY TO SHADE & LABEL	Shade in these colors. Label the individual mountains
	Cascade Mountain Range
	Mt. Rainier	△
	Mt. St. Helens	△
	Denali	△

Optional Cut & Paste Labels

| Cascade Mountains | Mt. Rainier |

| Mt. St. Helens | Denali |

27

Lesson 15

Now, let's trace, shade, & label!

	GEOGRAPHY TO DRAW & LABEL	SHADE IN THESE COLORS
	Huron	
	Ontario	
	Michigan	
	Erie	
	Superior	

Remember your acronym! HOMES

Optional Cut & Paste Labels

Lake Superior | Lake Michigan | Lake Huron | Lake Erie | Lake Ontario

Now, let's color, label and answer questions!

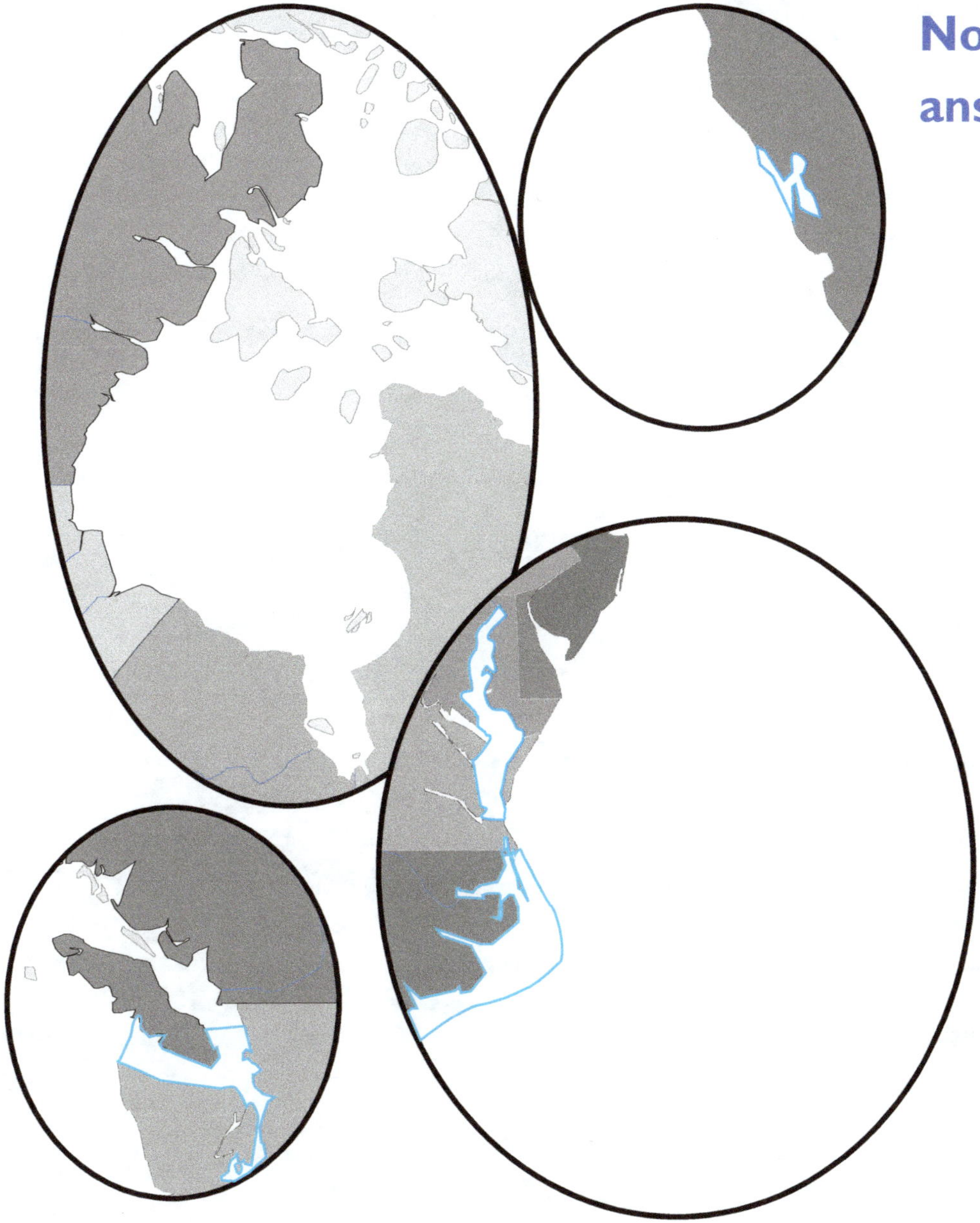

Lesson 16

Step 1: Color in the area of **Chesapeake Bay** with light blue and label.
Question: What two U.S. states does Chesapeake Bay border?

_____

Step 2: Color in the area of **Pamlico Sound** with light blue and label.
Question: What U.S. state does Pamlico Sound border?

_____

Question: Which coast is Chesapeake Bay and Pamlico Sound located? (circle one)

East Coast / West Coast

Step 3: Color in the area of **Hudson Bay** with light blue and label.
Question: What country in North America does Hudson Bay border?

_____

Step 4: Color in the area of **San Francisco Bay** with light blue and label.
Question: What U.S. state does San Francisco Bay border?

_____

Step 5: Color in the area of **Puget Sound** with light blue and label.
Question: What two North American countries does the Puget Sound border?

_____

| Chesapeake Bay | Hudson Bay | San Francisco Bay | Puget Sound | Pamlico Sound |

Now, let's trace & label!

Lesson 17

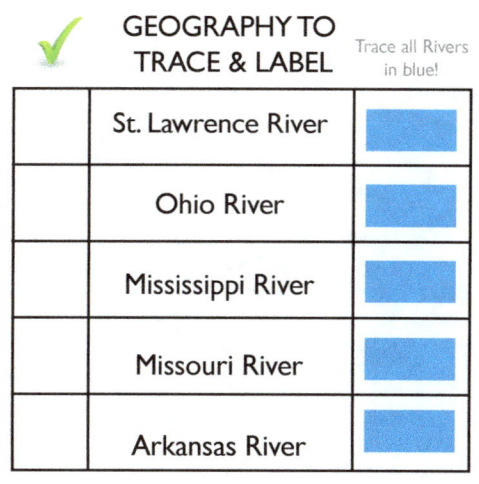

✓	GEOGRAPHY TO TRACE & LABEL	Trace all Rivers in blue!
	St. Lawrence River	
	Ohio River	
	Mississippi River	
	Missouri River	
	Arkansas River	

St. Lawrence River | Ohio River | Mississippi | Missouri River | Arkansas River

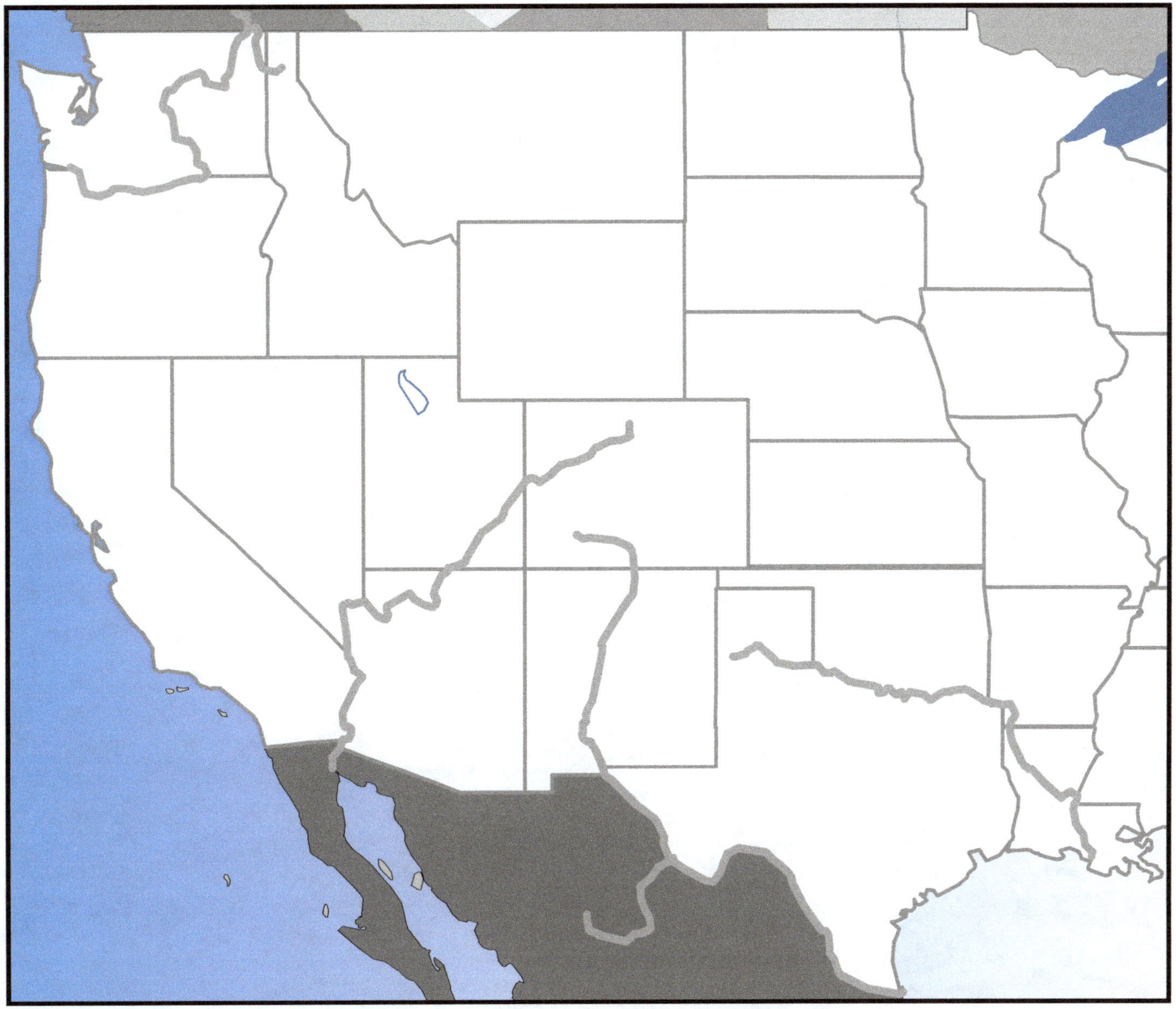

Lesson 18

Now, let's trace & label!

	GEOGRAPHY TO TRACE & LABEL	Trace all rivers in blue!
	Colorado River	
	Red River	
	Rio Grande River	
	Columbia River	
	Great Salt Lake	

Colorado River | Red River | Rio Grande River | Columbia River | Great Salt Lake

35

GEOGRAPHY TO TRACE & LABEL

Trace the trace in these colors

	Instruction	Color
☐	Starting in Maryland all the way to Illinois, draw the **Cumberland Road**	green
☐	Starting in the corner of Iowa and ending in Utah, draw the **Mormon Trail**	pink
☐	Starting in Missouri and ending in Oregon, draw the **Oregon Trail**	yellow
☐	Starting in Missouri and Kansas (two separate trail heads!) and ending in New Mexico, draw the **Santa Fe Trail**	dark green
☐	Starting in New Mexico and ending in Arizona, draw the **Gila Trail** (the "G" in Gila is pronounced like an "H")	purple
☐	Starting in New Mexico and ending in California, draw **The Old Spanish Trail**	brown
☐	Starting in Wyoming and ending in California, draw the **California Trail**	light blue

Lesson 19

Now, let's trace & label!

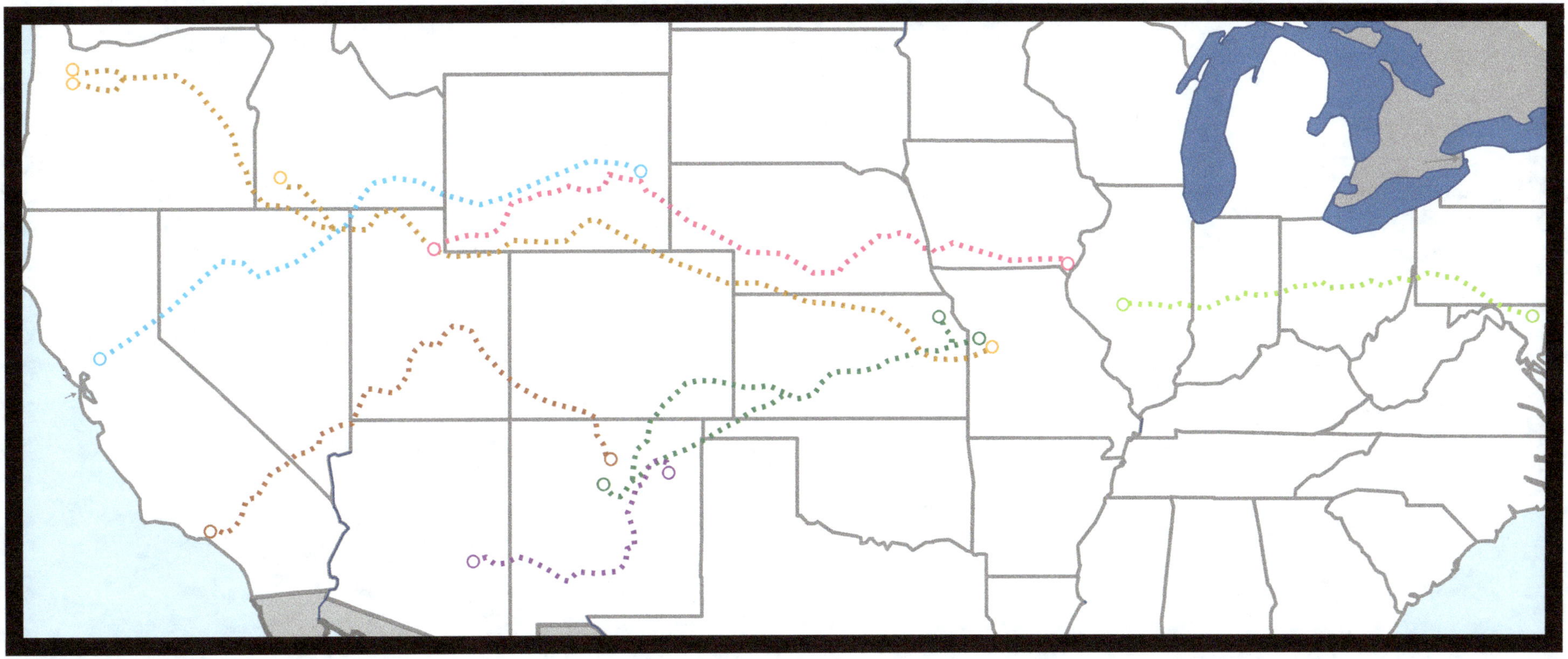

Optional Cut & Paste Labels

Cumberland Road | Santa Fe Trail | Mormon Trail | Gila Trail | Old Spanish Trail | California Trail | Oregon Trail

Lesson 20

Now, let's trace & label!

GEOGRAPHY TO DRAW & LABEL

Trace/Draw in these colors and/or shapes

	Beginning at the end of Lake Erie almost all the way to where Vermont and Massachusetts border New York for the **Erie Canal**.	
	Beginning at the tip of Delaware trace a portion of the **Pennsylvania Canal System**.	
	Beginning at the bottom of Massachusetts at Chesapeake Bay and draw the **Chesapeake & Ohio Canal** along the Virginia & Massachusetts and West Virginia & Massachusetts borders.	
	Beginning at the Lake Erie down through the state of Ohio for the **Ohio & Erie Canal**.	
	Left of the Ohio & Erie Canal draw a **blue line** beginning at the bottom/left of the state of Ohio moving upward almost to the top of the state of Ohio for the **Miami & Erie Canal**.	

Optional Cut & Paste Labels

------------ ✂ ---

| Erie Canal | Pennsylvania Canal | Chesapeake & Ohio Canal | Ohio & Erie Canal | Miami & Erie Canal |

39

Now, let's trace & label!

Lesson 21

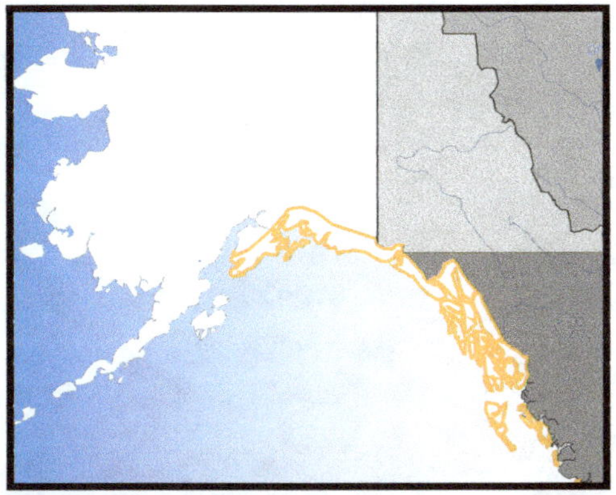

✓ GEOGRAPHY TO SHADE & LABEL

	Eastern Woodlands (Northeast)	
	Eastern Woodlands (Southeast)	
	Plains	
	Plateau	
	Northwest Coast	
	California	
	Giant Basin	
	Southwest	

Shade in These Colors

Optional Cut & Paste Labels

| Eastern Woodlands (NE) | Eastern Woodlands (SE) | Plains | Plateau | Northwest Coast | California | Great Basin | Southwest |

Now, let's trace, shade & label!

Lesson 22

✓	GEOGRAPHY TO TRACE, SHADE & LABEL	Trace & Shade in These Colors
	Mojave Desert	
	Sonoran Desert	
	Colorado Desert	
	Painted Desert	
	Great Salt Lake Desert	

Optional Cut & Paste Labels

Mojave Desert
Sonoran Desert
Colorado Desert
Painted Desert
Great Salt Lake Desert

Now, let's trace, shade, draw shapes, & label!

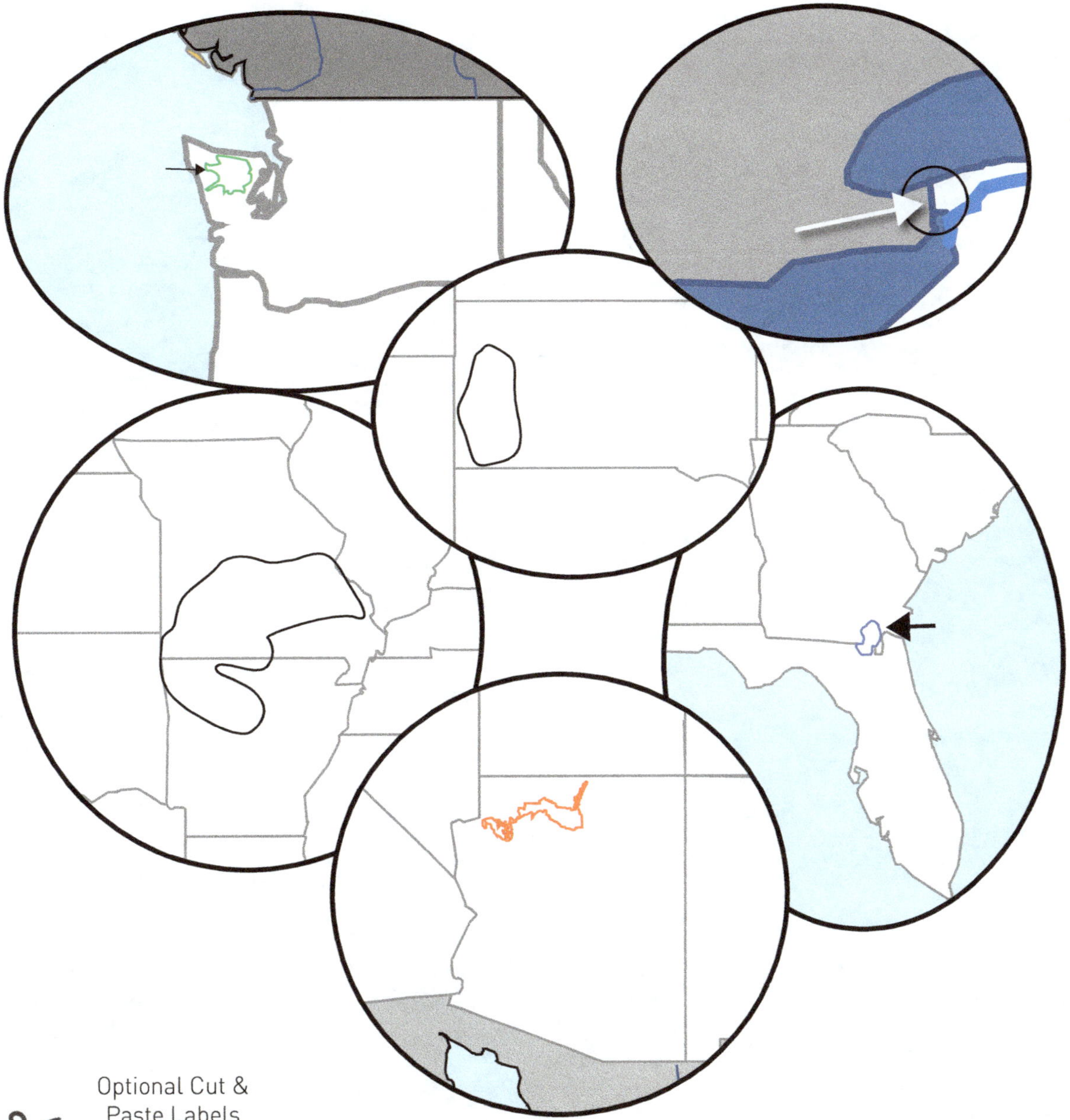

Lesson 23

GEOGRAPHY TO DRAW & LABEL

	Geography	Trace/Draw in these colors and/or shapes
	Grand Canyon	(yellow)
	Black Hills	▲▲▲
	Ozark Highlands	⌒⌒⌒
	Okefenokee Swamp	(dark blue)
	Olympic Rainforests	(green)
	Niagara Falls	(light blue)

Optional Cut & Paste Labels

Grand Canyon | Black Hills | Ozark Highlands | Okefenokee Swamp | Olympic Rainforests | Niagara Falls

45

Now, let's trace, shade, & label!

Lesson 24

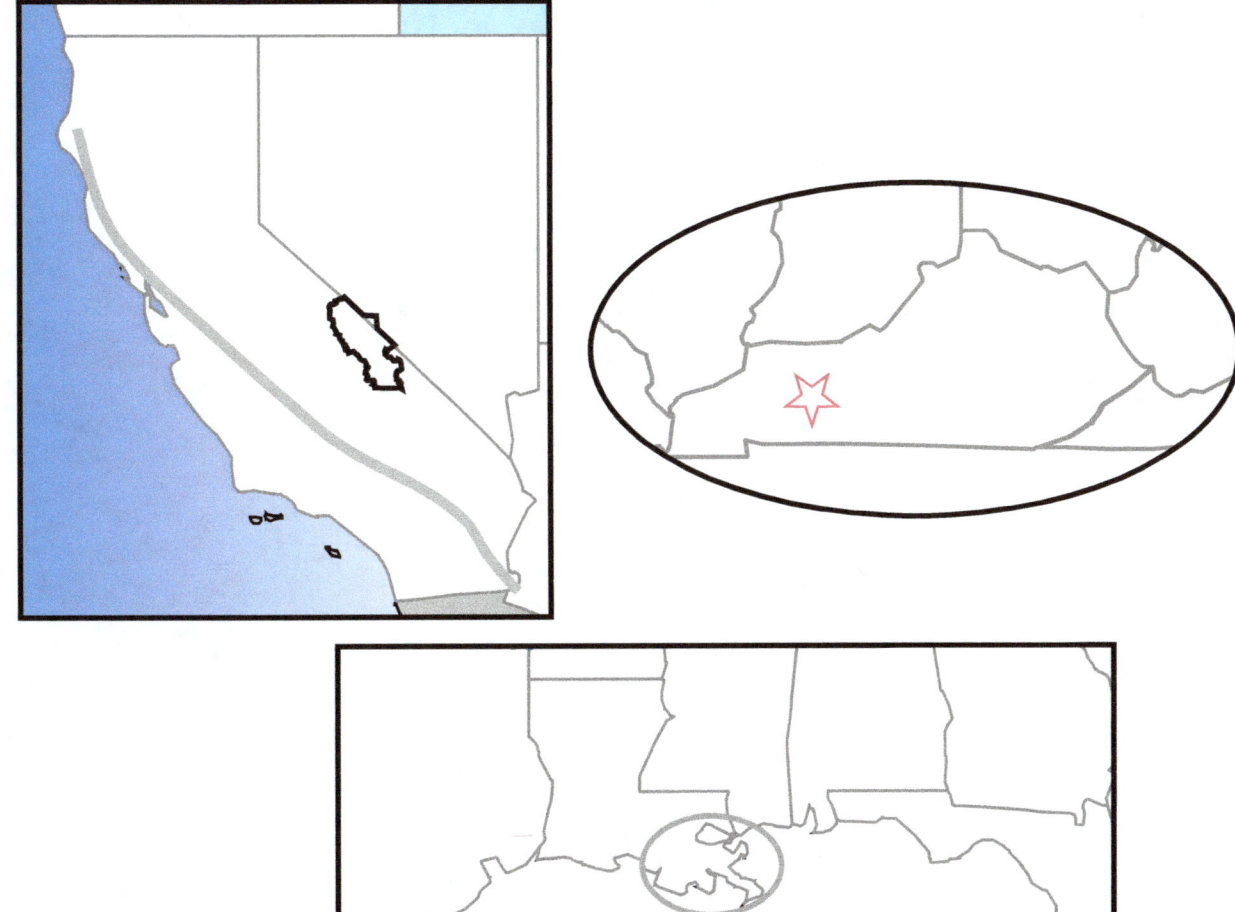

✓ GEOGRAPHY TO TRACE SHADE & LABEL

Trace & Shade in these colors and shapes

	Mississippi River Delta	
	Mammoth Cave	
	San Andreas Fault	
	Gulf of Mexico	
	Death Valley	

Optional Cut & Paste Labels

 -

| Mississippi River Delta | Mammoth Cave | San Andreas Fault | Gulf of Mexico | Death Valley |

47

Lava flowing into ocean - Kilauea Volcano, Hawaii-AdobeStock

TRUE REVIEW SCHEDULE

Please note two identical maps provided per page for twice weekly review.

Week # Review *Correlates with the Lesson you are currently studying, up to Lesson 24.**	Lessons Being Reviewed	Week # Review *Correlates with the Lesson you are currently studying, up to Lesson 24.**	Lessons Being Reviewed
1	1	16	10,11,12,13,14,15,16
2	1,2	17	11,12,13,14,15,16,17
3	1,2,3	18	12,13,14,15,16,17,18
4	1,2,3,4	19	13,14,15,16,17,18,19
5	1,2,3,4,5	20	14,15,16,17,18,19,20
6	1,2,3,4,5,6	21	15,16,17,18,19,20,21
7	1,2,3,4,5,6,7	22	16,17,18,19,20,21,22
8	2,3,4,5,6,7,8	23	17,18,19,20,21,22,23
9	3,4,5,6,7,8,9	24	18,19,20,21,22,23,24
10	4,5,6,7,8,9,10	25*	19,20,21,22,23,24
11	5,6,7,8,9,10,11	26*	20,21,22,23,24
12	6,7,8,9,10,11,12	27*	21,22,23,24
13	7,8,9,10,11,12,13	28*	22,23,24
14	8,9,10,11,12,13,14	29*	23,24
15	9,10,11,12,13,14,15	30*	24

*Weeks 25-30 cover the remaining lessons to give a true 6 week review of all lessons.

Tip!

All duplicated maps are back-to-back pages for the twice weekly review.

It is suggested posting this schedule so that you can easily reference which pages need to be done for the week.

MEMORIZATION THROUGH REPETITION

map sets completed twice weekly for a 6 week True Review!

TRUE REVIEW! Memorization Through Repetition

Do 2 Of This Map Per Lesson, This Map Is On The Backside Of This Page.

Week 1 REVIEW

Shade & Label all geography from Lesson 1

Augusta, Maine
Concord, New Hampshire
Boston, Massachusetts
Providence, Rhode Island
Hartford, Connecticut

2 TIPS!

The "Closer Look" map *(found within the Teaching & Student Resource / Tid-Bits Book)* **is a great resource when doing your TrueReview pages. The "Closer Look" map details just the geography that you need to review for this map. TIP #2:** Writing on maps can be hard and frustrating when there isn't enough room for the names. To fix this, take a separate sheet of paper and list the geographical names on it, giving each a number. Then, take those numbers and place them in the corresponding geographical area on this map. You can also write the geographic names in a clean space on this page and draw a clean line to the geography that the name belongs to.

TRUE REVIEW! Memorization Through Repetition

Do 2 Of This Map Per Lesson, This Map Is On The Backside Of This Page.

Week 1 REVIEW

Shade & Label all geography from Lesson 1

Augusta, Maine
Concord, New Hampshire
Boston, Massachusetts
Providence, Rhode Island
Hartford, Connecticut

2 TIPS!

The "Closer Look" map *(found within the Teaching & Student Resource / Tid-Bits Book)* **is a great resource when doing your TrueReview pages. The "Closer Look" map details just the geography that you need to review for this map. TIP #2:** Writing on maps can be hard and frustrating when there isn't enough room for the names. To fix this, take a separate sheet of paper and list the geographical names on it, giving each a number. Then, take those numbers and place them in the corresponding geographical area on this map. You can also write the geographic names in a clean space on this page and draw a clean line to the geography that the name belongs to.

TRUE REVIEW! Memorization Through Repetition

Do 2 Of This Map Per Lesson, This Map Is On The Backside Of This Page.

Week 2 REVIEW

Shade & Label all geography from Lessons 1 & 2

Augusta, Maine
Concord, New Hampshire
Boston, Massachusetts
Providence, Rhode Island
Hartford, Connecticut

Montpelier, Vermont
Albany, New York
Trenton, New Jersey
Harrisburg, Pennsylvania
Dover, Delaware

2 TIPS!

The "Closer Look" map *(found within the Teaching & Student Resource / Tid-Bits Book)* **is a great resource when doing your TrueReview pages. The "Closer Look" map details just the geography that you need to review for this map. TIP #2:** Writing on maps can be hard and frustrating when there isn't enough room for the names. To fix this, take a separate sheet of paper and list the geographical names on it, giving each a number. Then, take those numbers and place them in the corresponding geographical area on this map. You can also write the geographic names in a clean space on this page and draw a clean line to the geography that the name belongs to.

TRUE REVIEW! Memorization Through Repetition

Do 2 Of This Map Per Lesson, This Map Is On The Backside Of This Page.

Week 2 REVIEW

Shade & Label all geography from Lessons 1 & 2

Augusta, Maine
Concord, New Hampshire
Boston, Massachusetts
Providence, Rhode Island
Hartford, Connecticut

Montpelier, Vermont
Albany, New York
Trenton, New Jersey
Harrisburg, Pennsylvania
Dover, Delaware

2 TIPS!

The "Closer Look" map *(found within the Teaching & Student Resource / Tid-Bits Book)* **is a great resource when doing your TrueReview pages. The "Closer Look" map details just the geography that you need to review for this map. TIP #2:** Writing on maps can be hard and frustrating when there isn't enough room for the names. To fix this, take a separate sheet of paper and list the geographical names on it, giving each a number. Then, take those numbers and place them in the corresponding geographical area on this map. You can also write the geographic names in a clean space on this page and draw a clean line to the geography that the name belongs to.

TRUE REVIEW! Memorization Through Repetition

Do 2 Of This Map Per Lesson, This Map Is On The Backside Of This Page.

Week 3 REVIEW

Shade & Label all geography from Lessons 1, 2, & 3

Augusta, Maine
Concord, New Hampshire
Boston, Massachusetts
Providence, Rhode Island
Hartford, Connecticut

Montpelier, Vermont
Albany, New York
Trenton, New Jersey
Harrisburg, Pennsylvania
Dover, Delaware

Annapolis, Maryland
Richmond, Virginia
Charleston, West Virginia
Raleigh, North Carolina
Columbia, South Carolina
Washington D.C.

2 TIPS!

The "**Closer Look**" **map** *(found within the Teaching & Student Resource / Tid-Bits Book)* **is a great resource when doing your TrueReview pages. The "Closer Look" map details just the geography that you need to review for this map. TIP #2:** Writing on maps can be hard and frustrating when there isn't enough room for the names. To fix this, take a separate sheet of paper and list the geographical names on it, giving each a number. Then, take those numbers and place them in the corresponding geographical area on this map. You can also write the geographic names in a clean space on this page and draw a clean line to the geography that the name belongs to.

TRUE REVIEW! Memorization Through Repetition

Do 2 Of This Map Per Lesson, This Map Is On The Backside Of This Page.

Week 3 REVIEW

Shade & Label all geography from Lessons 1, 2, & 3

Augusta, Maine
Concord, New Hampshire
Boston, Massachusetts
Providence, Rhode Island
Hartford, Connecticut

Montpelier, Vermont
Albany, New York
Trenton, New Jersey
Harrisburg, Pennsylvania
Dover, Delaware

Annapolis, Maryland
Richmond, Virginia
Charleston, West Virginia
Raleigh, North Carolina
Columbia, South Carolina
Washington D.C.

2 TIPS!

The "Closer Look" map *(found within the Teaching & Student Resource / Tid-Bits Book)* **is a great resource when doing your TrueReview pages. The "Closer Look" map details just the geography that you need to review for this map. TIP #2:** Writing on maps can be hard and frustrating when there isn't enough room for the names. To fix this, take a separate sheet of paper and list the geographical names on it, giving each a number. Then, take those numbers and place them in the corresponding geographical area on this map. You can also write the geographic names in a clean space on this page and draw a clean line to the geography that the name belongs to.

TRUE REVIEW! Memorization Through Repetition

Do 2 Of This Map Per Lesson, This Map Is On The Backside Of This Page.

Week 4 REVIEW

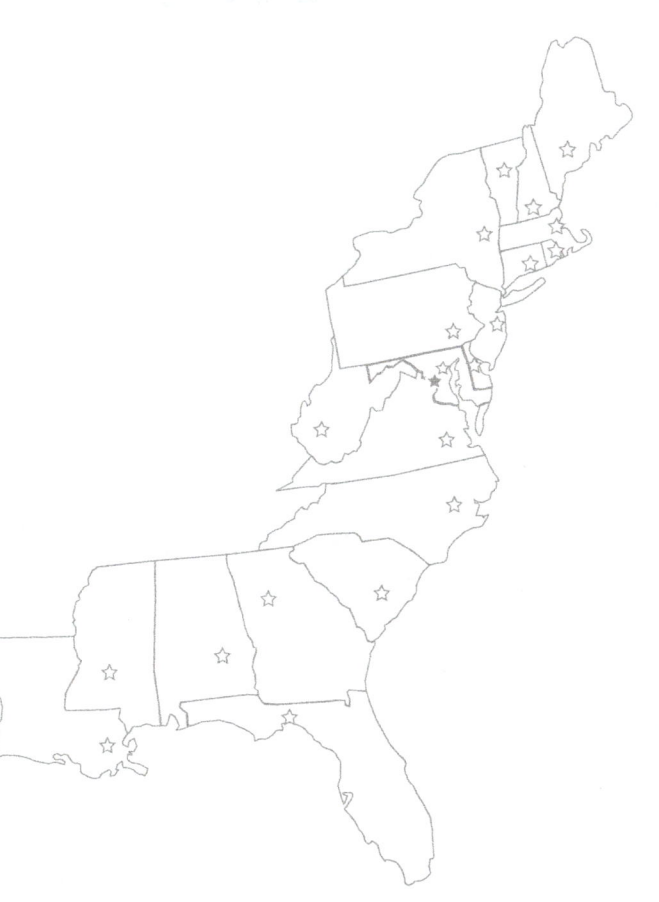

Shade & Label all geography from Lessons 1, 2, 3, & 4

Augusta, Maine
Concord, New Hampshire
Boston, Massachusetts
Providence, Rhode Island
Hartford, Connecticut

Montpelier, Vermont
Albany, New York
Trenton, New Jersey
Harrisburg, Pennsylvania
Dover, Delaware

Annapolis, Maryland
Richmond, Virginia
Charleston, West Virginia
Raleigh, North Carolina
Columbia, South Carolina
Washington D.C.

Atlanta, Georgia
Tallahassee, Florida
Montgomery, Alabama
Jackson, Mississippi
Baton Rouge, Louisiana

2 TIPS!

The "Closer Look" map *(found within the Teaching & Student Resource / Tid-Bits Book)* **is a great resource when doing your TrueReview pages. The "Closer Look" map details just the geography that you need to review for this map. TIP #2:** Writing on maps can be hard and frustrating when there isn't enough room for the names. To fix this, take a separate sheet of paper and list the geographical names on it, giving each a number. Then, take those numbers and place them in the corresponding geographical area on this map. You can also write the geographic names in a clean space on this page and draw a clean line to the geography that the name belongs to.

TRUE REVIEW! Memorization Through Repetition

Do 2 Of This Map Per Lesson, This Map Is On The Backside Of This Page.

Week 4 REVIEW

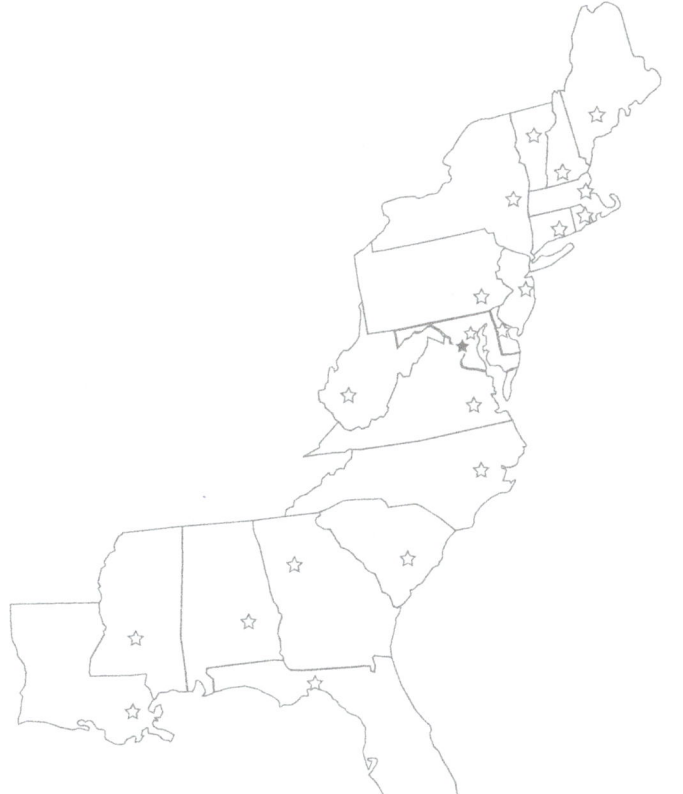

Shade & Label all geography from Lessons 1, 2, 3, & 4

Augusta, Maine
Concord, New Hampshire
Boston, Massachusetts
Providence, Rhode Island
Hartford, Connecticut

Montpelier, Vermont
Albany, New York
Trenton, New Jersey
Harrisburg, Pennsylvania
Dover, Delaware

Annapolis, Maryland
Richmond, Virginia
Charleston, West Virginia
Raleigh, North Carolina
Columbia, South Carolina
Washington D.C.

Atlanta, Georgia
Tallahassee, Florida
Montgomery, Alabama
Jackson, Mississippi
Baton Rouge, Louisiana

2 TIPS!

The "Closer Look" map *(found within the Teaching & Student Resource / Tid-Bits Book)* **is a great resource when doing your TrueReview pages. The "Closer Look" map details just the geography that you need to review for this map. TIP #2:** Writing on maps can be hard and frustrating when there isn't enough room for the names. To fix this, take a separate sheet of paper and list the geographical names on it, giving each a number. Then, take those numbers and place them in the corresponding geographical area on this map. You can also write the geographic names in a clean space on this page and draw a clean line to the geography that the name belongs to.

TRUE REVIEW! Memorization Through Repetition

Do 2 Of This Map Per Lesson, This Map Is On The Backside Of This Page.

Week 5 REVIEW

Shade & Label all geography from Lessons 1, 2, 3, 4 & 5

Augusta, Maine
Concord, New Hampshire
Boston, Massachusetts
Providence, Rhode Island
Hartford, Connecticut

Montpelier, Vermont
Albany, New York
Trenton, New Jersey
Harrisburg, Pennsylvania
Dover, Delaware

Annapolis, Maryland
Richmond, Virginia
Charleston, West Virginia
Raleigh, North Carolina
Columbia, South Carolina
Washington D.C.

Atlanta, Georgia
Tallahassee, Florida
Montgomery, Alabama
Jackson, Mississippi
Baton Rouge, Louisiana

Lansing, Michigan
Columbus, Ohio
Indianapolis, Indiana
Frankfort, Kentucky
Nashville, Tennessee

2 TIPS!

The "Closer Look" map *(found within the Teaching & Student Resource / Tid-Bits Book)* **is a great resource when doing your TrueReview pages. The "Closer Look" map details just the geography that you need to review for this map. TIP #2:** Writing on maps can be hard and frustrating when there isn't enough room for the names. To fix this, take a separate sheet of paper and list the geographical names on it, giving each a number. Then, take those numbers and place them in the corresponding geographical area on this map. You can also write the geographic names in a clean space on this page and draw a clean line to the geography that the name belongs to.

TRUE REVIEW! Memorization Through Repetition

Do 2 Of This Map Per Lesson, This Map Is On The Backside Of This Page.

Week 5 REVIEW

Shade & Label all geography from Lessons 1, 2, 3, 4 & 5

Augusta, Maine
Concord, New Hampshire
Boston, Massachusetts
Providence, Rhode Island
Hartford, Connecticut

Montpelier, Vermont
Albany, New York
Trenton, New Jersey
Harrisburg, Pennsylvania
Dover, Delaware

Annapolis, Maryland
Richmond, Virginia
Charleston, West Virginia
Raleigh, North Carolina
Columbia, South Carolina
Washington D.C.

Atlanta, Georgia
Tallahassee, Florida
Montgomery, Alabama
Jackson, Mississippi
Baton Rouge, Louisiana

Lansing, Michigan
Columbus, Ohio
Indianapolis, Indiana
Frankfort, Kentucky
Nashville, Tennessee

2 TIPS!

The "Closer Look" map *(found within the Teaching & Student Resource / Tid-Bits Book)* **is a great resource when doing your TrueReview pages. The "Closer Look" map details just the geography that you need to review for this map. TIP #2:** Writing on maps can be hard and frustrating when there isn't enough room for the names. To fix this, take a separate sheet of paper and list the geographical names on it, giving each a number. Then, take those numbers and place them in the corresponding geographical area on this map. You can also write the geographic names in a clean space on this page and draw a clean line to the geography that the name belongs to.

TRUE REVIEW! Memorization Through Repetition

Do 2 Of This Map Per Lesson, This Map Is On The Backside Of This Page.

Week 6 REVIEW

Shade & Label all geography from Lessons 1, 2, 3, 4, 5 & 6

Augusta, Maine
Concord, New Hampshire
Boston, Massachusetts
Providence, Rhode Island
Hartford, Connecticut

Montpelier, Vermont
Albany, New York
Trenton, New Jersey
Harrisburg, Pennsylvania
Dover, Delaware

Annapolis, Maryland
Richmond, Virginia
Charleston, West Virginia
Raleigh, North Carolina
Columbia, South Carolina
Washington D.C.

Atlanta, Georgia
Tallahassee, Florida
Montgomery, Alabama
Jackson, Mississippi
Baton Rouge, Louisiana

Lansing, Michigan
Columbus, Ohio
Indianapolis, Indiana
Frankfort, Kentucky
Nashville, Tennessee

Madison, Wisconsin
Springfield, Illinois
Des Moines, Iowa
Jefferson City, Missouri
Little Rock, Arkansas

2 TIPS!

The "Closer Look" map *(found within the Teaching & Student Resource / Tid-Bits Book)* **is a great resource when doing your TrueReview pages. The "Closer Look" map details just the geography that you need to review for this map. TIP #2:** Writing on maps can be hard and frustrating when there isn't enough room for the names. To fix this, take a separate sheet of paper and list the geographical names on it, giving each a number. Then, take those numbers and place them in the corresponding geographical area on this map. You can also write the geographic names in a clean space on this page and draw a clean line to the geography that the name belongs to.

TRUE REVIEW! Memorization Through Repetition

Do 2 Of This Map Per Lesson, This Map Is On The Backside Of This Page.

Week 6 REVIEW

Shade & Label all geography from Lessons 1, 2, 3,4, 5 & 6

Augusta, Maine
Concord, New Hampshire
Boston, Massachusetts
Providence, Rhode Island
Hartford, Connecticut

Montpelier, Vermont
Albany, New York
Trenton, New Jersey
Harrisburg, Pennsylvania
Dover, Delaware

Annapolis, Maryland
Richmond, Virginia
Charleston, West Virginia
Raleigh, North Carolina
Columbia, South Carolina
Washington D.C.

Atlanta, Georgia
Tallahassee, Florida
Montgomery, Alabama
Jackson, Mississippi
Baton Rouge, Louisiana

Lansing, Michigan
Columbus, Ohio
Indianapolis, Indiana
Frankfort, Kentucky
Nashville, Tennessee

Madison, Wisconsin
Springfield, Illinois
Des Moines, Iowa
Jefferson City, Missouri
Little Rock, Arkansas

2 TIPS!

The "Closer Look" map *(found within the Teaching & Student Resource / Tid-Bits Book)* **is a great resource when doing your TrueReview pages. The "Closer Look" map details just the geography that you need to review for this map. TIP #2:** Writing on maps can be hard and frustrating when there isn't enough room for the names. To fix this, take a separate sheet of paper and list the geographical names on it, giving each a number. Then, take those numbers and place them in the corresponding geographical area on this map. You can also write the geographic names in a clean space on this page and draw a clean line to the geography that the name belongs to.

TRUE REVIEW! Memorization Through Repetition

Do 2 Of This Map Per Lesson, This Map Is On The Backside Of This Page.

Week 7 REVIEW

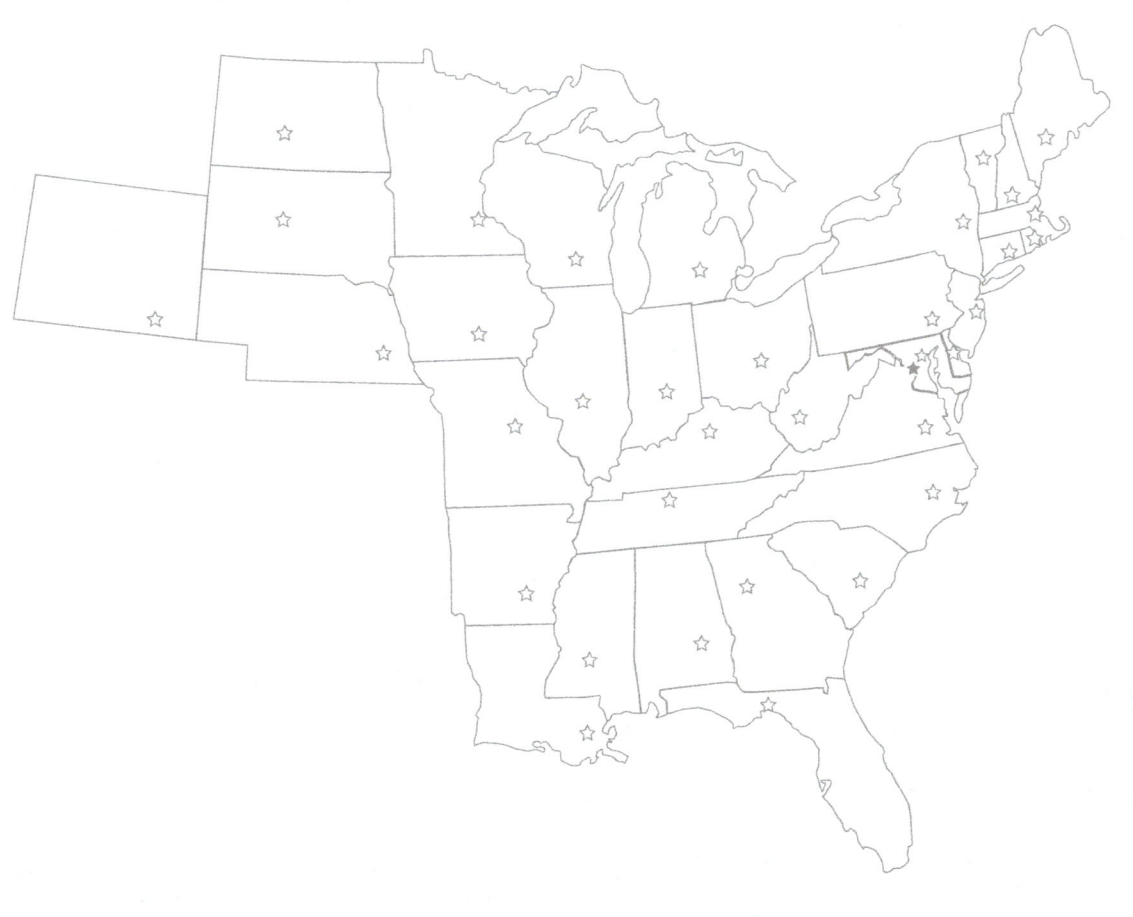

Shade & Label all geography from Lessons 1, 2, 3, 4, 5, 6, & 7:

Augusta, Maine
Concord, New Hampshire
Boston, Massachusetts
Providence, Rhode Island
Hartford, Connecticut

Montpelier, Vermont
Albany, New York
Trenton, New Jersey
Harrisburg, Pennsylvania
Dover, Delaware

Annapolis, Maryland
Richmond, Virginia
Charleston, West Virginia
Raleigh, North Carolina
Columbia, South Carolina
Washington D.C.

Atlanta, Georgia
Tallahassee, Florida
Montgomery, Alabama
Jackson, Mississippi
Baton Rouge, Louisiana

Lansing, Michigan
Columbus, Ohio
Indianapolis, Indiana
Frankfort, Kentucky
Nashville, Tennessee

Madison, Wisconsin
Springfield, Illinois
Des Moines, Iowa
Jefferson City, Missouri
Little Rock, Arkansas

St. Paul, Minnesota
Bismarck, North Dakota
Pierre, South Dakota
Cheyenne, Wyoming
Lincoln, Nebraska

2 TIPS!

The "Closer Look" map *(found within the Teaching & Student Resource / Tid-Bits Book)* **is a great resource when doing your TrueReview pages. The "Closer Look" map details just the geography that you need to review for this map. TIP #2:** Writing on maps can be hard and frustrating when there isn't enough room for the names. To fix this, take a separate sheet of paper and list the geographical names on it, giving each a number. Then, take those numbers and place them in the corresponding geographical area on this map. You can also write the geographic names in a clean space on this page and draw a clean line to the geography that the name belongs to.

TRUE REVIEW! Memorization Through Repetition

Do 2 Of This Map Per Lesson, This Map Is On The Backside Of This Page.

Week 7 REVIEW

Shade & Label all geography from Lessons 1, 2, 3,4, 5, 6, & 7:

Augusta, Maine
Concord, New Hampshire
Boston, Massachusetts
Providence, Rhode Island
Hartford, Connecticut

Montpelier, Vermont
Albany, New York
Trenton, New Jersey
Harrisburg, Pennsylvania
Dover, Delaware

Annapolis, Maryland
Richmond, Virginia
Charleston, West Virginia
Raleigh, North Carolina
Columbia, South Carolina
Washington D.C.

Atlanta, Georgia
Tallahassee, Florida
Montgomery, Alabama
Jackson, Mississippi
Baton Rouge, Louisiana

Lansing, Michigan
Columbus, Ohio
Indianapolis, Indiana
Frankfort, Kentucky
Nashville, Tennessee

Madison, Wisconsin
Springfield, Illinois
Des Moines, Iowa
Jefferson City, Missouri
Little Rock, Arkansas

St. Paul, Minnesota
Bismarck, North Dakota
Pierre, South Dakota
Cheyenne, Wyoming
Lincoln, Nebraska

2 TIPS!

The "Closer Look" map *(found within the Teaching & Student Resource / Tid-Bits Book)* **is a great resource when doing your TrueReview pages. The "Closer Look" map details just the geography that you need to review for this map. TIP #2:** Writing on maps can be hard and frustrating when there isn't enough room for the names. To fix this, take a separate sheet of paper and list the geographical names on it, giving each a number. Then, take those numbers and place them in the corresponding geographical area on this map. You can also write the geographic names in a clean space on this page and draw a clean line to the geography that the name belongs to.

TRUE REVIEW! Memorization Through Repetition

Do 2 Of This Map Per Lesson, This Map Is On The Backside Of This Page.

Week 8 REVIEW

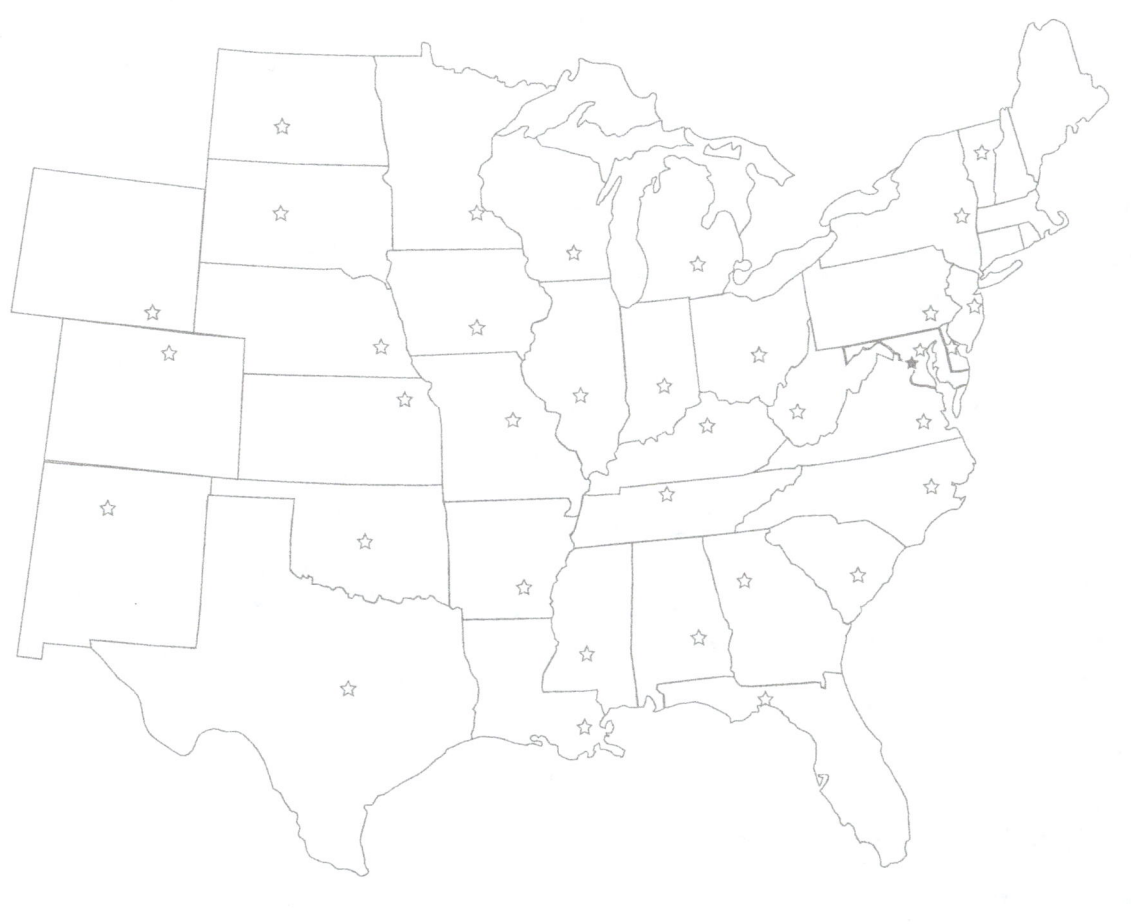

Shade & Label all geography from Lessons 2, 3, 4, 5, 6, 7, 8:

Montpelier, Vermont
Albany, New York
Trenton, New Jersey
Harrisburg, Pennsylvania
Dover, Delaware

Annapolis, Maryland
Richmond, Virginia
Charleston, West Virginia
Raleigh, North Carolina
Columbia, South Carolina
Washington D.C.

Atlanta, Georgia
Tallahassee, Florida
Montgomery, Alabama
Jackson, Mississippi
Baton Rouge, Louisiana

Lansing, Michigan
Columbus, Ohio
Indianapolis, Indiana
Frankfort, Kentucky
Nashville, Tennessee

Madison, Wisconsin
Springfield, Illinois
Des Moines, Iowa
Jefferson City, Missouri
Little Rock, Arkansas

St. Paul, Minnesota
Bismarck, North Dakota
Pierre, South Dakota
Cheyenne, Wyoming
Lincoln, Nebraska

Topeka, Kansas
Oklahoma City, Oklahoma
Austin, Texas
Denver, Colorado
Santa Fe, New Mexico

2 TIPS!

The "Closer Look" map *(found within the Teaching & Student Resource / Tid-Bits Book)* **is a great resource when doing your TrueReview pages. The "Closer Look" map details just the geography that you need to review for this map. TIP #2:** Writing on maps can be hard and frustrating when there isn't enough room for the names. To fix this, take a separate sheet of paper and list the geographical names on it, giving each a number. Then, take those numbers and place them in the corresponding geographical area on this map. You can also write the geographic names in a clean space on this page and draw a clean line to the geography that the name belongs to.

TRUE REVIEW! Memorization Through Repetition

Do 2 Of This Map Per Lesson, This Map Is On The Backside Of This Page.

Week 8 REVIEW

Shade & Label all geography from Lessons 2, 3,4, 5, 6, 7, 8:

Montpelier, Vermont
Albany, New York
Trenton, New Jersey
Harrisburg, Pennsylvania
Dover, Delaware

Annapolis, Maryland
Richmond, Virginia
Charleston, West Virginia
Raleigh, North Carolina
Columbia, South Carolina
Washington D.C.

Atlanta, Georgia
Tallahassee, Florida
Montgomery, Alabama
Jackson, Mississippi
Baton Rouge, Louisiana

Lansing, Michigan
Columbus, Ohio
Indianapolis, Indiana
Frankfort, Kentucky
Nashville, Tennessee

Madison, Wisconsin
Springfield, Illinois
Des Moines, Iowa
Jefferson City, Missouri
Little Rock, Arkansas

St. Paul, Minnesota
Bismarck, North Dakota
Pierre, South Dakota
Cheyenne, Wyoming
Lincoln, Nebraska

Topeka, Kansas
Oklahoma City, Oklahoma
Austin, Texas
Denver, Colorado
Santa Fe, New Mexico

2 TIPS!

The "Closer Look" map *(found within the Teaching & Student Resource / Tid-Bits Book)* **is a great resource when doing your TrueReview pages. The "Closer Look" map details just the geography that you need to review for this map. TIP #2:** Writing on maps can be hard and frustrating when there isn't enough room for the names. To fix this, take a separate sheet of paper and list the geographical names on it, giving each a number. Then, take those numbers and place them in the corresponding geographical area on this map. You can also write the geographic names in a clean space on this page and draw a clean line to the geography that the name belongs to.

TRUE REVIEW! Memorization Through Repetition

Do 2 Of This Map Per Lesson, This Map Is On The Backside Of This Page.

Week 9 REVIEW

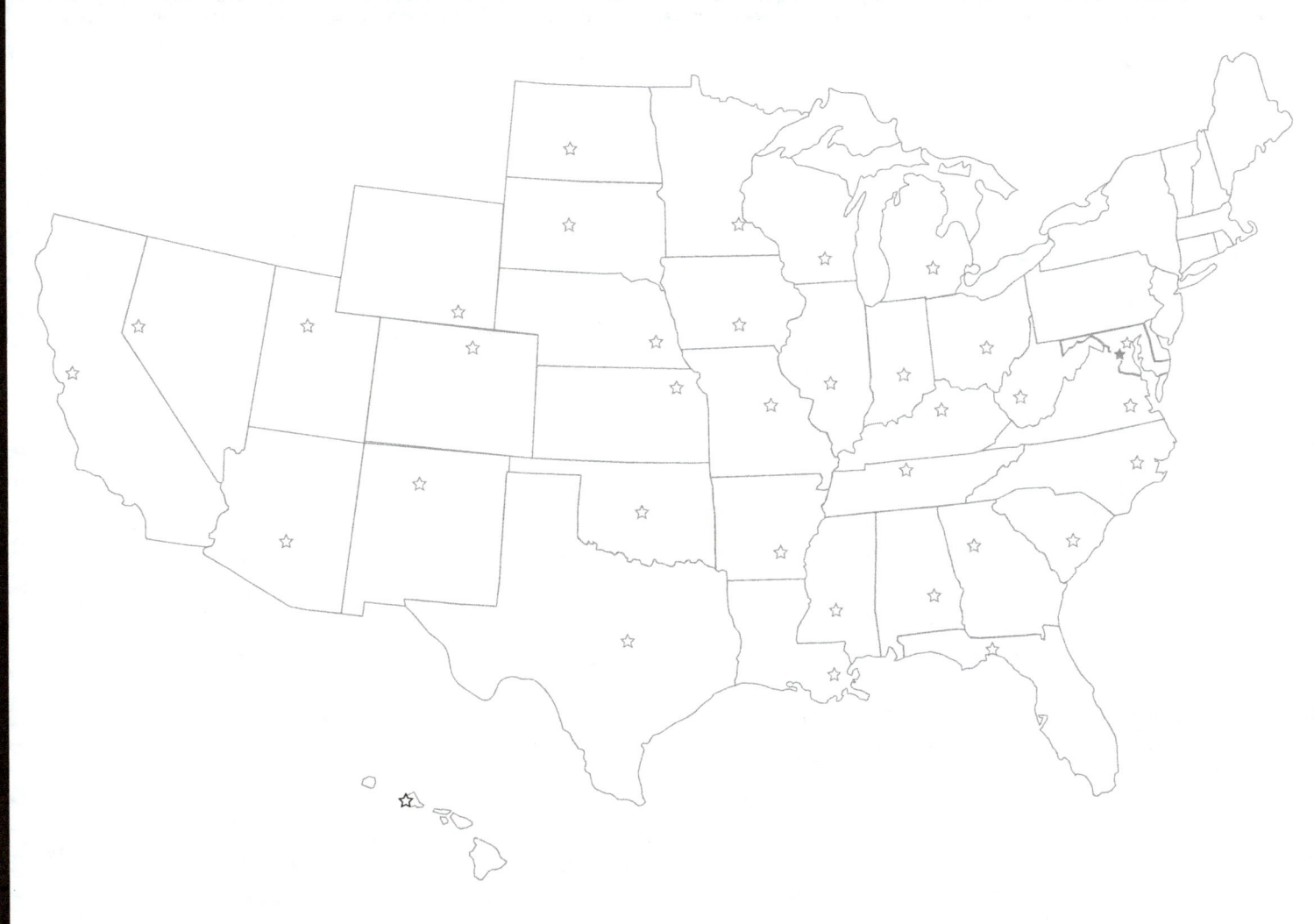

Shade & Label all geography from Lessons 3, 4, 5, 6 7, 8, & 9:

Annapolis, Maryland
Richmond, Virginia
Charleston, West Virginia
Raleigh, North Carolina
Columbia, South Carolina
Washington D.C.

Atlanta, Georgia
Tallahassee, Florida
Montgomery, Alabama
Jackson, Mississippi
Baton Rouge, Louisiana

Lansing, Michigan
Columbus, Ohio
Indianapolis, Indiana
Frankfort, Kentucky
Nashville, Tennessee

Madison, Wisconsin
Springfield, Illinois
Des Moines, Iowa
Jefferson City, Missouri
Little Rock, Arkansas

St. Paul, Minnesota
Bismarck, North Dakota
Pierre, South Dakota
Cheyenne, Wyoming
Lincoln, Nebraska

Topeka, Kansas
Oklahoma City, Oklahoma
Austin, Texas
Denver, Colorado
Santa Fe, New Mexico

Salt Lake City, Utah
Phoenix, Arizona
Carson City, Nevada
Sacramento, California
Honolulu, Hawaii

2 TIPS!

The "Closer Look" map *(found within the Teaching & Student Resource / Tid-Bits Book)* **is a great resource when doing your TrueReview pages. The "Closer Look" map details just the geography that you need to review for this map. TIP #2:** Writing on maps can be hard and frustrating when there isn't enough room for the names. To fix this, take a separate sheet of paper and list the geographical names on it, giving each a number. Then, take those numbers and place them in the corresponding geographical area on this map. You can also write the geographic names in a clean space on this page and draw a clean line to the geography that the name belongs to.

TRUE REVIEW! Memorization Through Repetition

Do 2 Of This Map Per Lesson, This Map Is On The Backside Of This Page.

Week 9 REVIEW

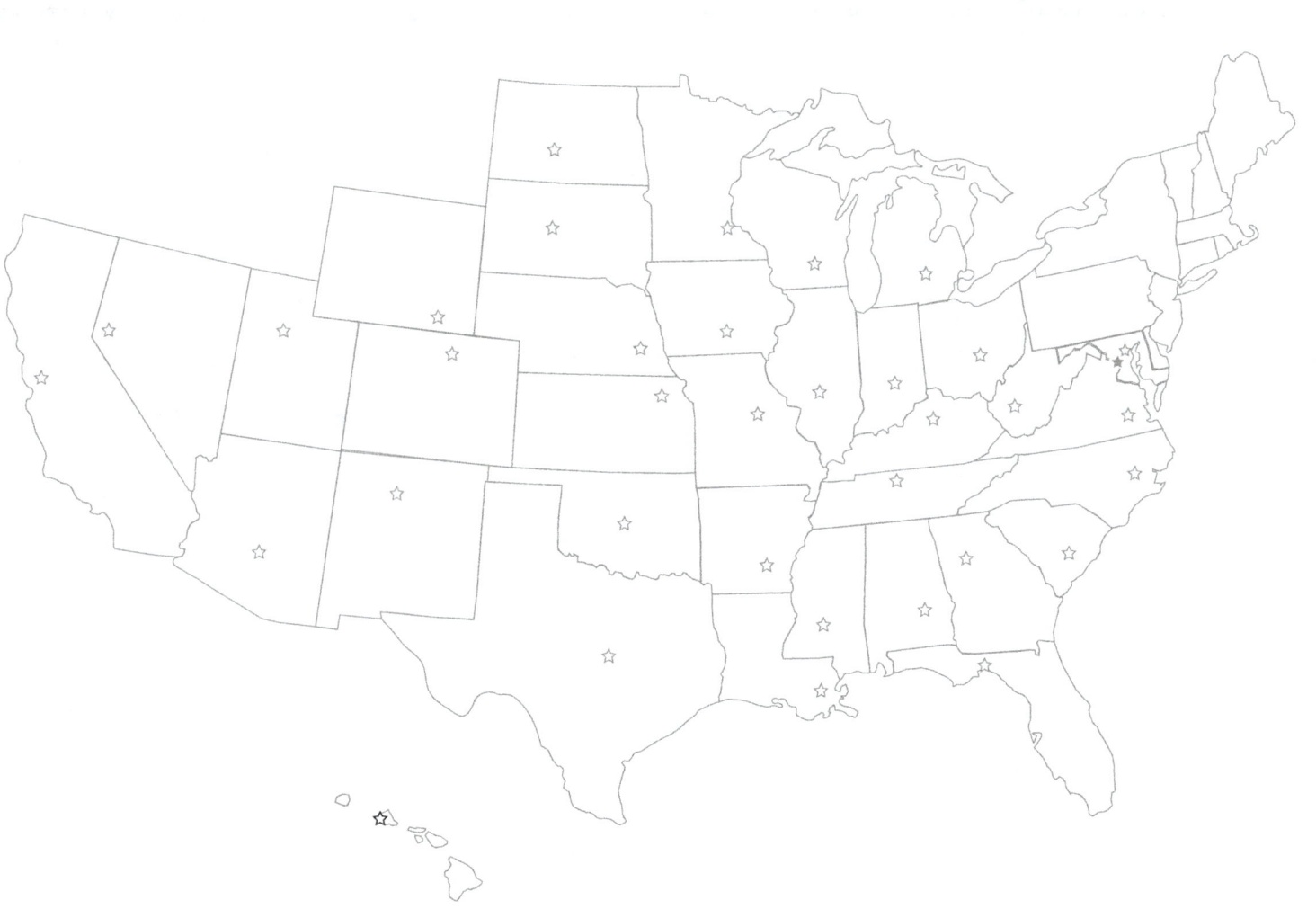

Shade & Label all geography from Lessons 3, 4, 5, 6 7, 8, & 9:

Annapolis, Maryland
Richmond, Virginia
Charleston, West Virginia
Raleigh, North Carolina
Columbia, South Carolina
Washington D.C.

Atlanta, Georgia
Tallahassee, Florida
Montgomery, Alabama
Jackson, Mississippi
Baton Rouge, Louisiana

Lansing, Michigan
Columbus, Ohio
Indianapolis, Indiana
Frankfort, Kentucky
Nashville, Tennessee

Madison, Wisconsin
Springfield, Illinois
Des Moines, Iowa
Jefferson City, Missouri
Little Rock, Arkansas

St. Paul, Minnesota
Bismarck, North Dakota
Pierre, South Dakota
Cheyenne, Wyoming
Lincoln, Nebraska

Topeka, Kansas
Oklahoma City, Oklahoma
Austin, Texas
Denver, Colorado
Santa Fe, New Mexico

Salt Lake City, Utah
Phoenix, Arizona
Carson City, Nevada
Sacramento, California
Honolulu, Hawaii

2 TIPS!

The "Closer Look" map *(found within the Teaching & Student Resource / Tid-Bits Book)* **is a great resource when doing your TrueReview pages. The "Closer Look" map details just the geography that you need to review for this map. TIP #2:** Writing on maps can be hard and frustrating when there isn't enough room for the names. To fix this, take a separate sheet of paper and list the geographical names on it, giving each a number. Then, take those numbers and place them in the corresponding geographical area on this map. You can also write the geographic names in a clean space on this page and draw a clean line to the geography that the name belongs to.

TRUE REVIEW! Memorization Through Repetition — Week 10 REVIEW

Do 2 Of This Map Per Lesson, This Map Is On The Backside Of This Page.

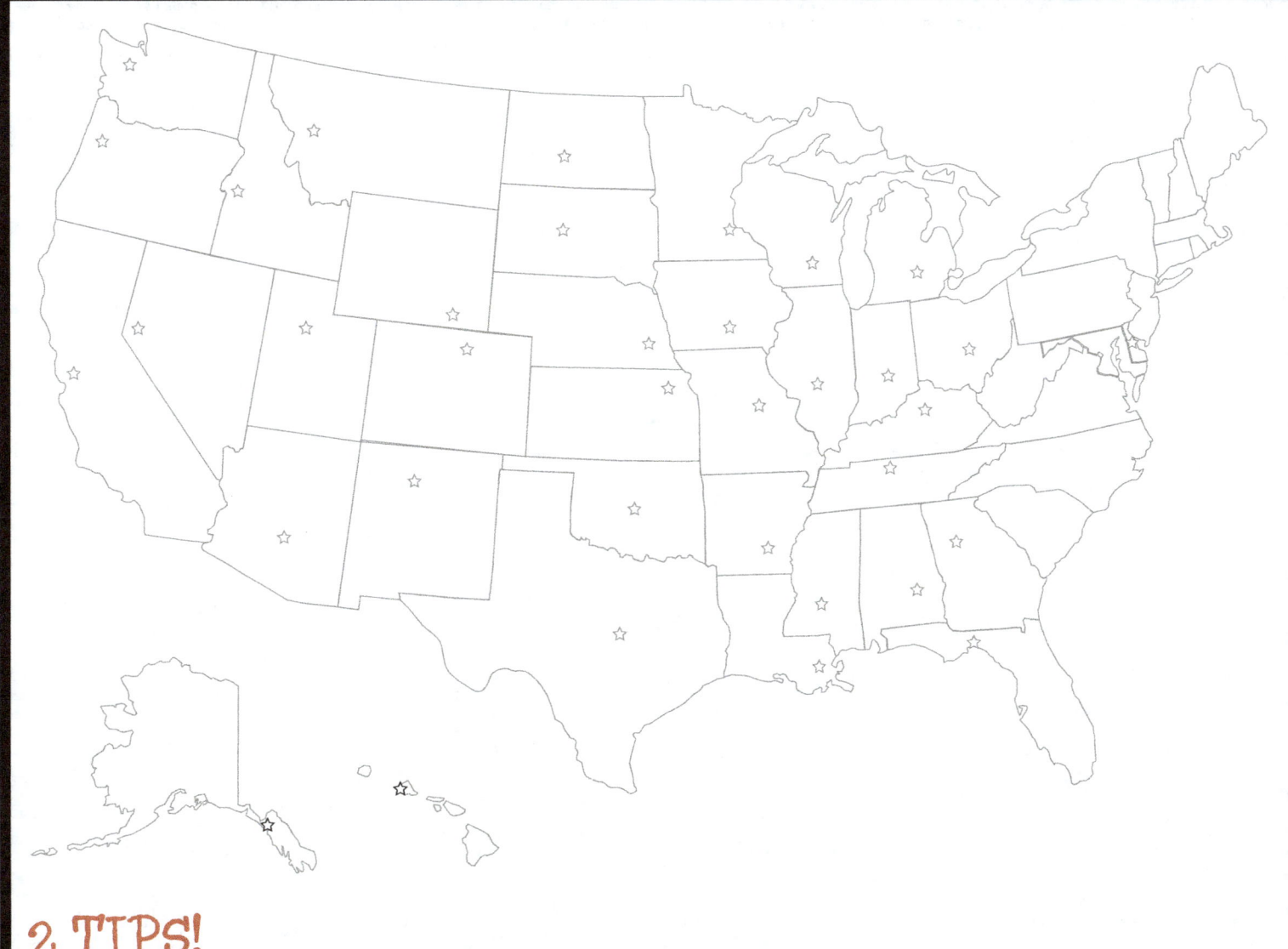

Shade & Label all geography from Lessons 4, 5, 6, 7, 8, 9, & 10:

Atlanta, Georgia
Tallahassee, Florida
Montgomery, Alabama
Jackson, Mississippi
Baton Rouge, Louisiana

Lansing, Michigan
Columbus, Ohio
Indianapolis, Indiana
Frankfort, Kentucky
Nashville, Tennessee

Madison, Wisconsin
Springfield, Illinois
Des Moines, Iowa
Jefferson City, Missouri
Little Rock, Arkansas

St. Paul, Minnesota
Bismarck, North Dakota
Pierre, South Dakota
Cheyenne, Wyoming
Lincoln, Nebraska

Topeka, Kansas
Oklahoma City, Oklahoma
Austin, Texas
Denver, Colorado
Santa Fe, New Mexico

Salt Lake City, Utah
Phoenix, Arizona
Carson City, Nevada
Sacramento, California
Honolulu, Hawaii

Helena, Montana
Boise, Idaho
Olympia, Washington
Salem, Oregon
Juneau, Alaska

2 TIPS!

The "Closer Look" map *(found within the Teaching & Student Resource / Tid-Bits Book)* **is a great resource when doing your TrueReview pages. The "Closer Look" map details just the geography that you need to review for this map. TIP #2:** Writing on maps can be hard and frustrating when there isn't enough room for the names. To fix this, take a separate sheet of paper and list the geographical names on it, giving each a number. Then, take those numbers and place them in the corresponding geographical area on this map. You can also write the geographic names in a clean space on this page and draw a clean line to the geography that the name belongs to.

TRUE REVIEW! Memorization Through Repetition
Do 2 Of This Map Per Lesson, This Map Is On The Backside Of This Page.
Week 10 REVIEW

Shade & Label all geography from Lessons 4, 5, 6, 7 8, 9, & 10:

Atlanta, Georgia
Tallahassee, Florida
Montgomery, Alabama
Jackson, Mississippi
Baton Rouge, Louisiana

Lansing, Michigan
Columbus, Ohio
Indianapolis, Indiana
Frankfort, Kentucky
Nashville, Tennessee

Madison, Wisconsin
Springfield, Illinois
Des Moines, Iowa
Jefferson City, Missouri
Little Rock, Arkansas

St. Paul, Minnesota
Bismarck, North Dakota
Pierre, South Dakota
Cheyenne, Wyoming
Lincoln, Nebraska

Topeka, Kansas
Oklahoma City, Oklahoma
Austin, Texas
Denver, Colorado
Santa Fe, New Mexico

Salt Lake City, Utah
Phoenix, Arizona
Carson City, Nevada
Sacramento, California
Honolulu, Hawaii

Helena, Montana
Boise, Idaho
Olympia, Washington
Salem, Oregon
Juneau, Alaska

2 TIPS!

The "Closer Look" map *(found within the Teaching & Student Resource / Tid-Bits Book)* **is a great resource when doing your TrueReview pages. The "Closer Look" map details just the geography that you need to review for this map. TIP #2:** Writing on maps can be hard and frustrating when there isn't enough room for the names. To fix this, take a separate sheet of paper and list the geographical names on it, giving each a number. Then, take those numbers and place them in the corresponding geographical area on this map. You can also write the geographic names in a clean space on this page and draw a clean line to the geography that the name belongs to.

TRUE REVIEW! Memorization Through Repetition

Do 2 Of This Map Per Lesson, This Map Is On The Backside Of This Page.

Week 11 REVIEW

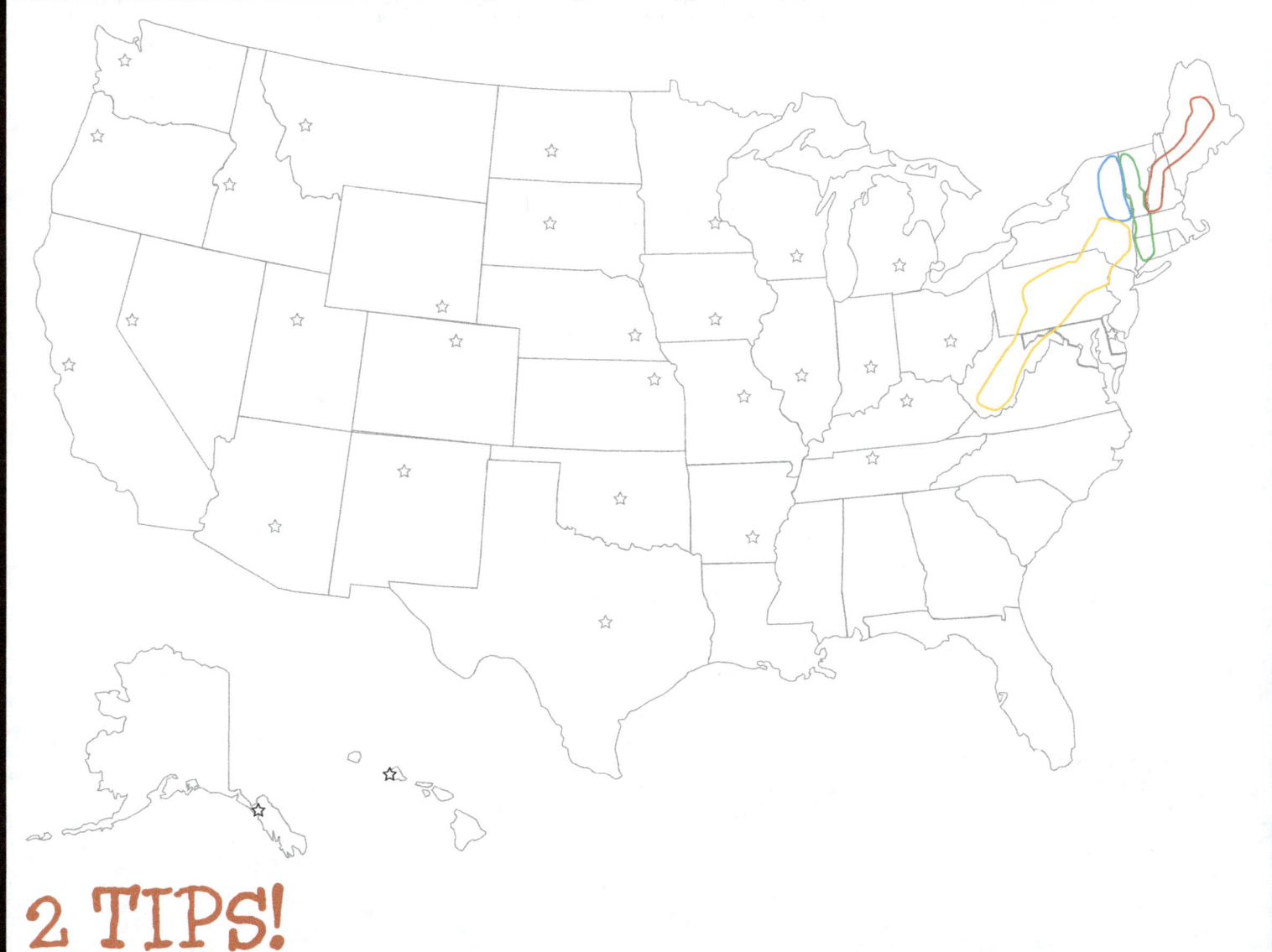

Shade & Label all geography from Lessons 5, 6, 7, 8, 9, 10, & 11:

Lansing, Michigan
Columbus, Ohio
Indianapolis, Indiana
Frankfort, Kentucky
Nashville, Tennessee

Madison, Wisconsin
Springfield, Illinois
Des Moines, Iowa
Jefferson City, Missouri
Little Rock, Arkansas

St. Paul, Minnesota
Bismarck, North Dakota
Pierre, South Dakota
Cheyenne, Wyoming
Lincoln, Nebraska

Topeka, Kansas
Oklahoma City, Oklahoma
Austin, Texas
Denver, Colorado
Santa Fe, New Mexico

Salt Lake City, Utah
Phoenix, Arizona
Carson City, Nevada
Sacramento, California
Honolulu, Hawaii

Helena, Montana
Boise, Idaho
Olympia, Washington
Salem, Oregon
Juneau, Alaska

White Mountains
Green Mountains
Adirondack Mountains
Allegheny Mountains

2 TIPS!

The "Closer Look" map *(found within the Teaching & Student Resource / Tid-Bits Book)* **is a great resource when doing your TrueReview pages. The "Closer Look" map details just the geography that you need to review for this map. TIP #2:** Writing on maps can be hard and frustrating when there isn't enough room for the names. To fix this, take a separate sheet of paper and list the geographical names on it, giving each a number. Then, take those numbers and place them in the corresponding geographical area on this map. You can also write the geographic names in a clean space on this page and draw a clean line to the geography that the name belongs to.

TRUE REVIEW! Memorization Through Repetition

Do 2 Of This Map Per Lesson, This Map Is On The Backside Of This Page.

Week 11 REVIEW

Shade & Label all geography from Lessons 5, 6, 7 8, 9, 10, & 11:

Lansing, Michigan
Columbus, Ohio
Indianapolis, Indiana
Frankfort, Kentucky
Nashville, Tennessee

Madison, Wisconsin
Springfield, Illinois
Des Moines, Iowa
Jefferson City, Missouri
Little Rock, Arkansas

St. Paul, Minnesota
Bismarck, North Dakota
Pierre, South Dakota
Cheyenne, Wyoming
Lincoln, Nebraska

Topeka, Kansas
Oklahoma City, Oklahoma
Austin, Texas
Denver, Colorado
Santa Fe, New Mexico

Salt Lake City, Utah
Phoenix, Arizona
Carson City, Nevada
Sacramento, California
Honolulu, Hawaii

Helena, Montana
Boise, Idaho
Olympia, Washington
Salem, Oregon
Juneau, Alaska

White Mountains
Green Mountains
Adirondack Mountains
Allegheny Mountains

2 TIPS!

The "Closer Look" map *(found within the Teaching & Student Resource / Tid-Bits Book)* **is a great resource when doing your TrueReview pages. The "Closer Look" map details just the geography that you need to review for this map. TIP #2:** Writing on maps can be hard and frustrating when there isn't enough room for the names. To fix this, take a separate sheet of paper and list the geographical names on it, giving each a number. Then, take those numbers and place them in the corresponding geographical area on this map. You can also write the geographic names in a clean space on this page and draw a clean line to the geography that the name belongs to.

TRUE REVIEW! Memorization Through Repetition — Week 12 REVIEW

Do 2 Of This Map Per Lesson, This Map Is On The Backside Of This Page.

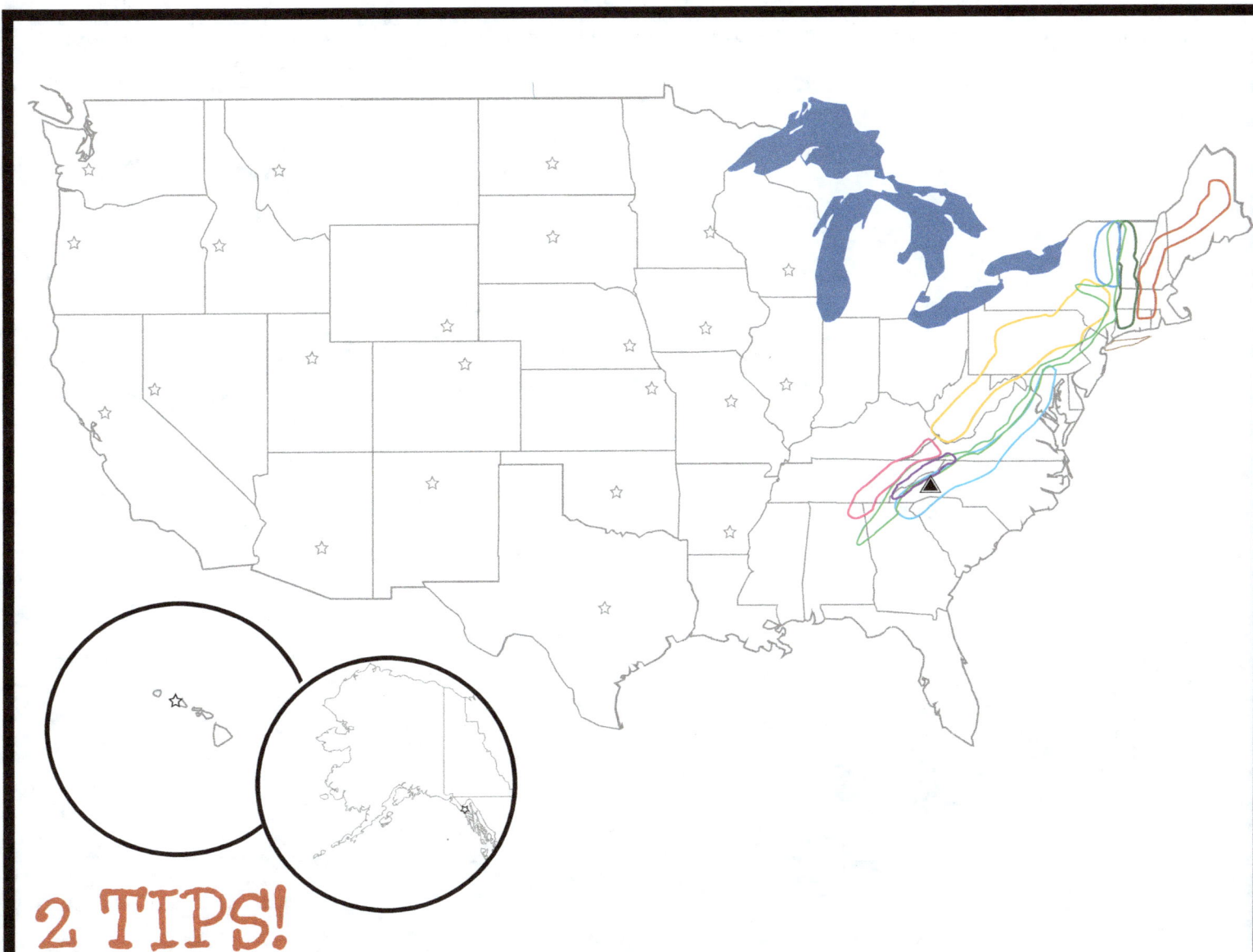

Shade & Label all geography from Lessons 6, 7 8, 9, 10, 11, & 12:

Madison, Wisconsin
Springfield, Illinois
Des Moines, Iowa
Jefferson City, Missouri
Little Rock, Arkansas

St. Paul, Minnesota
Bismarck, North Dakota
Pierre, South Dakota
Cheyenne, Wyoming
Lincoln, Nebraska

Topeka, Kansas
Oklahoma City, Oklahoma
Austin, Texas
Denver, Colorado
Santa Fe, New Mexico

Salt Lake City, Utah
Phoenix, Arizona
Carson City, Nevada
Sacramento, California
Honolulu, Hawaii

Helena, Montana
Boise, Idaho
Olympia, Washington
Salem, Oregon
Juneau, Alaska

White Mountains
Green Mountains
Adirondack Mountains
Allegheny Mountains

The Great Valley
Blue Ridge Mountains
Great Smoky Mountains
Cumberland Mountains
Mt. Mitchell

2 TIPS!

The "Closer Look" map *(found within the Teaching & Student Resource / Tid-Bits Book)* **is a great resource when doing your TrueReview pages. The "Closer Look" map details just the geography that you need to review for this map.** **TIP #2:** Writing on maps can be hard and frustrating when there isn't enough room for the names. To fix this, take a separate sheet of paper and list the geographical names on it, giving each a number. Then, take those numbers and place them in the corresponding geographical area on this map. You can also write the geographic names in a clean space on this page and draw a clean line to the geography that the name belongs to.

TRUE REVIEW! Memorization Through Repetition

Do 2 Of This Map Per Lesson, This Map Is On The Backside Of This Page.

Week 12 REVIEW

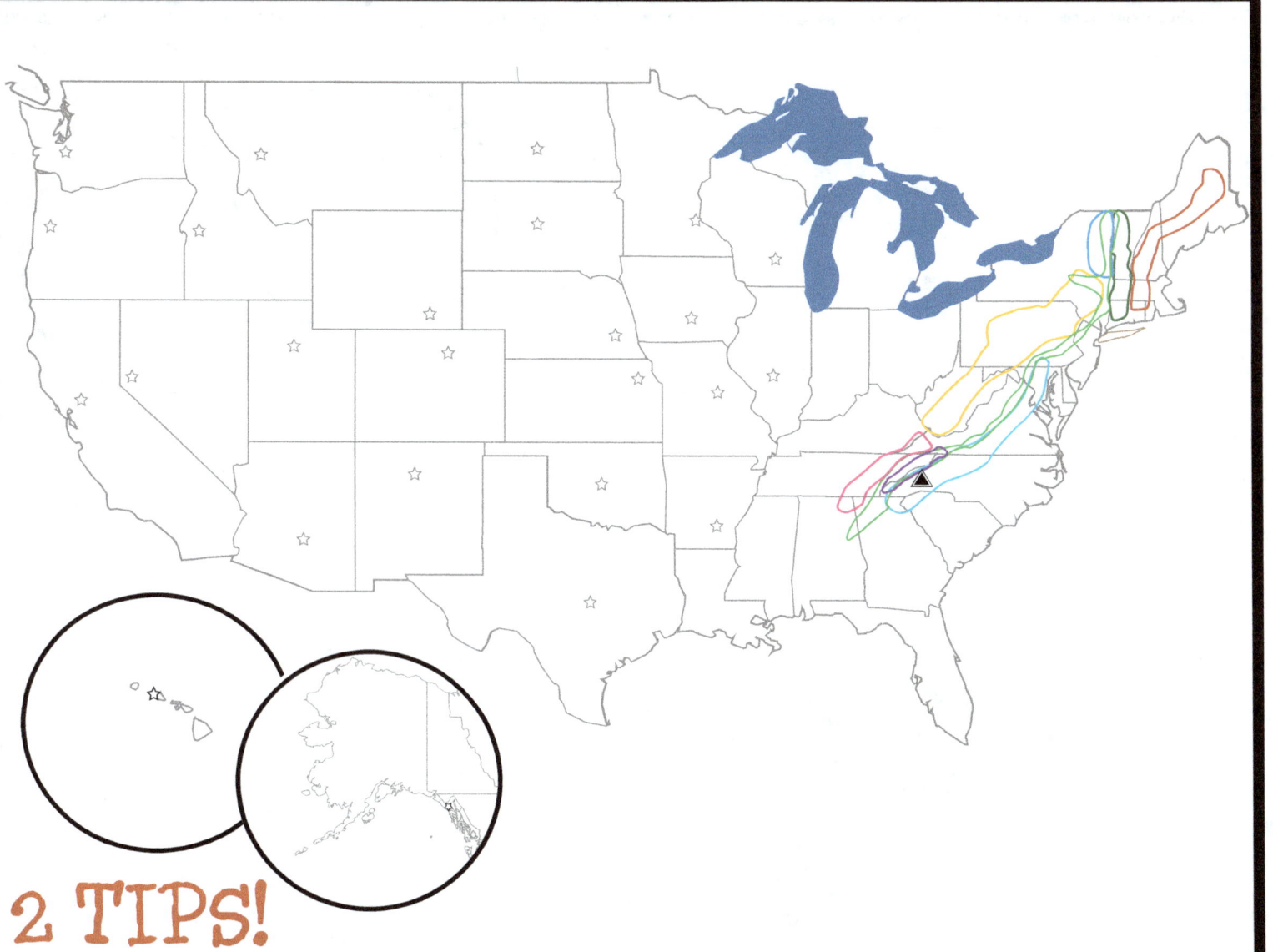

Shade & Label all geography from Lessons 6, 7 8, 9, 10, 11, & 12:

Madison, Wisconsin
Springfield, Illinois
Des Moines, Iowa
Jefferson City, Missouri
Little Rock, Arkansas

St. Paul, Minnesota
Bismarck, North Dakota
Pierre, South Dakota
Cheyenne, Wyoming
Lincoln, Nebraska

Topeka, Kansas
Oklahoma City, Oklahoma
Austin, Texas
Denver, Colorado
Santa Fe, New Mexico

Salt Lake City, Utah
Phoenix, Arizona
Carson City, Nevada
Sacramento, California
Honolulu, Hawaii

Helena, Montana
Boise, Idaho
Olympia, Washington
Salem, Oregon
Juneau, Alaska

White Mountains
Green Mountains
Adirondack Mountains
Allegheny Mountains

The Great Valley
Blue Ridge Mountains
Great Smoky Mountains
Cumberland Mountains
Mt. Mitchell

2 TIPS!

The "Closer Look" map *(found within the Teaching & Student Resource / Tid-Bits Book)* **is a great resource when doing your TrueReview pages. The "Closer Look" map details just the geography that you need to review for this map. TIP #2:** Writing on maps can be hard and frustrating when there isn't enough room for the names. To fix this, take a separate sheet of paper and list the geographical names on it, giving each a number. Then, take those numbers and place them in the corresponding geographical area on this map. You can also write the geographic names in a clean space on this page and draw a clean line to the geography that the name belongs to.

TRUE REVIEW! Memorization Through Repetition

Do 2 Of This Map Per Lesson, This Map Is On The Backside Of This Page.

Week 13 REVIEW

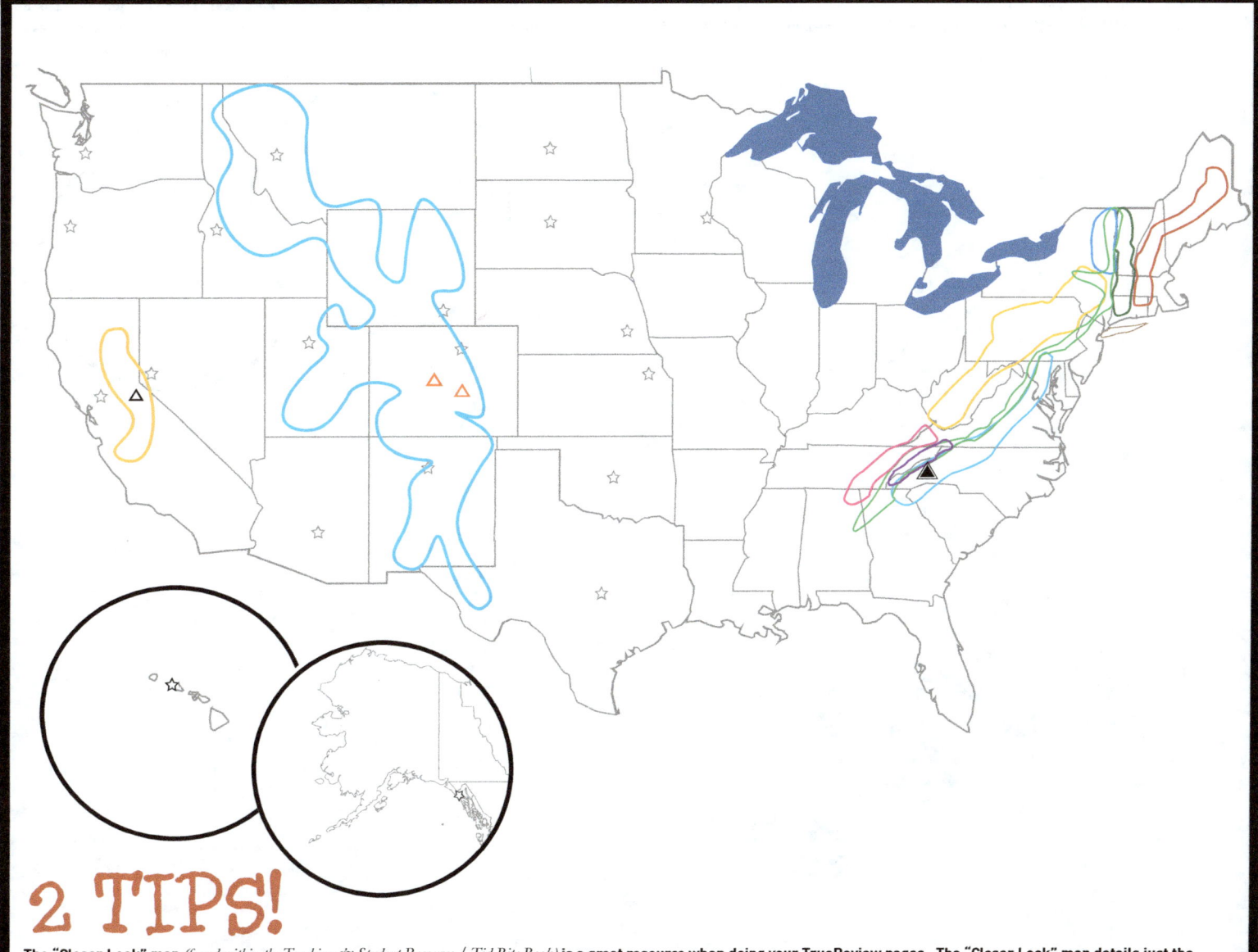

Shade & Label all geography from Lessons 7, 8, 9, 10, 11, 12, & 13:

St. Paul, Minnesota
Bismarck, North Dakota
Pierre, South Dakota
Cheyenne, Wyoming
Lincoln, Nebraska

Topeka, Kansas
Oklahoma City, Oklahoma
Austin, Texas
Denver, Colorado
Santa Fe, New Mexico

Salt Lake City, Utah
Phoenix, Arizona
Carson City, Nevada
Sacramento, California
Honolulu, Hawaii

Helena, Montana
Boise, Idaho
Olympia, Washington
Salem, Oregon
Juneau, Alaska

White Mountains
Green Mountains
Adirondack Mountains
Allegheny Mountains

The Great Valley
Blue Ridge Mountains
Great Smoky Mountains
Cumberland Mountains
Mt. Mitchell

Rocky Mountains
Pikes Peak
Mt. Elbert
Sierra Nevada
Mt. Whitney

2 TIPS!

The "Closer Look" map *(found within the Teaching & Student Resource / Tid-Bits Book)* **is a great resource when doing your TrueReview pages. The "Closer Look" map details just the geography that you need to review for this map. TIP #2:** Writing on maps can be hard and frustrating when there isn't enough room for the names. To fix this, take a separate sheet of paper and list the geographical names on it, giving each a number. Then, take those numbers and place them in the corresponding geographical area on this map. You can also write the geographic names in a clean space on this page and draw a clean line to the geography that the name belongs to.

TRUE REVIEW! Memorization Through Repetition

Do 2 Of This Map Per Lesson, This Map Is On The Backside Of This Page.

Week 13 REVIEW

Shade & Label all geography from Lessons 7, 8, 9, 10, 11, 12, & 13:

St. Paul, Minnesota
Bismarck, North Dakota
Pierre, South Dakota
Cheyenne, Wyoming
Lincoln, Nebraska

Topeka, Kansas
Oklahoma City, Oklahoma
Austin, Texas
Denver, Colorado
Santa Fe, New Mexico

Salt Lake City, Utah
Phoenix, Arizona
Carson City, Nevada
Sacramento, California
Honolulu, Hawaii

Helena, Montana
Boise, Idaho
Olympia, Washington
Salem, Oregon
Juneau, Alaska

White Mountains
Green Mountains
Adirondack Mountains
Allegheny Mountains

The Great Valley
Blue Ridge Mountains
Great Smoky Mountains
Cumberland Mountains
Mt. Mitchell

Rocky Mountains
Pikes Peak
Mt. Elbert
Sierra Nevada
Mt. Whitney

2 TIPS!

The "Closer Look" map *(found within the Teaching & Student Resource / Tid-Bits Book)* **is a great resource when doing your TrueReview pages. The "Closer Look" map details just the geography that you need to review for this map. TIP #2:** Writing on maps can be hard and frustrating when there isn't enough room for the names. To fix this, take a separate sheet of paper and list the geographical names on it, giving each a number. Then, take those numbers and place them in the corresponding geographical area on this map. You can also write the geographic names in a clean space on this page and draw a clean line to the geography that the name belongs to.

TRUE REVIEW! Memorization Through Repetition — Week 14 REVIEW

Do 2 Of This Map Per Lesson, This Map Is On The Backside Of This Page.

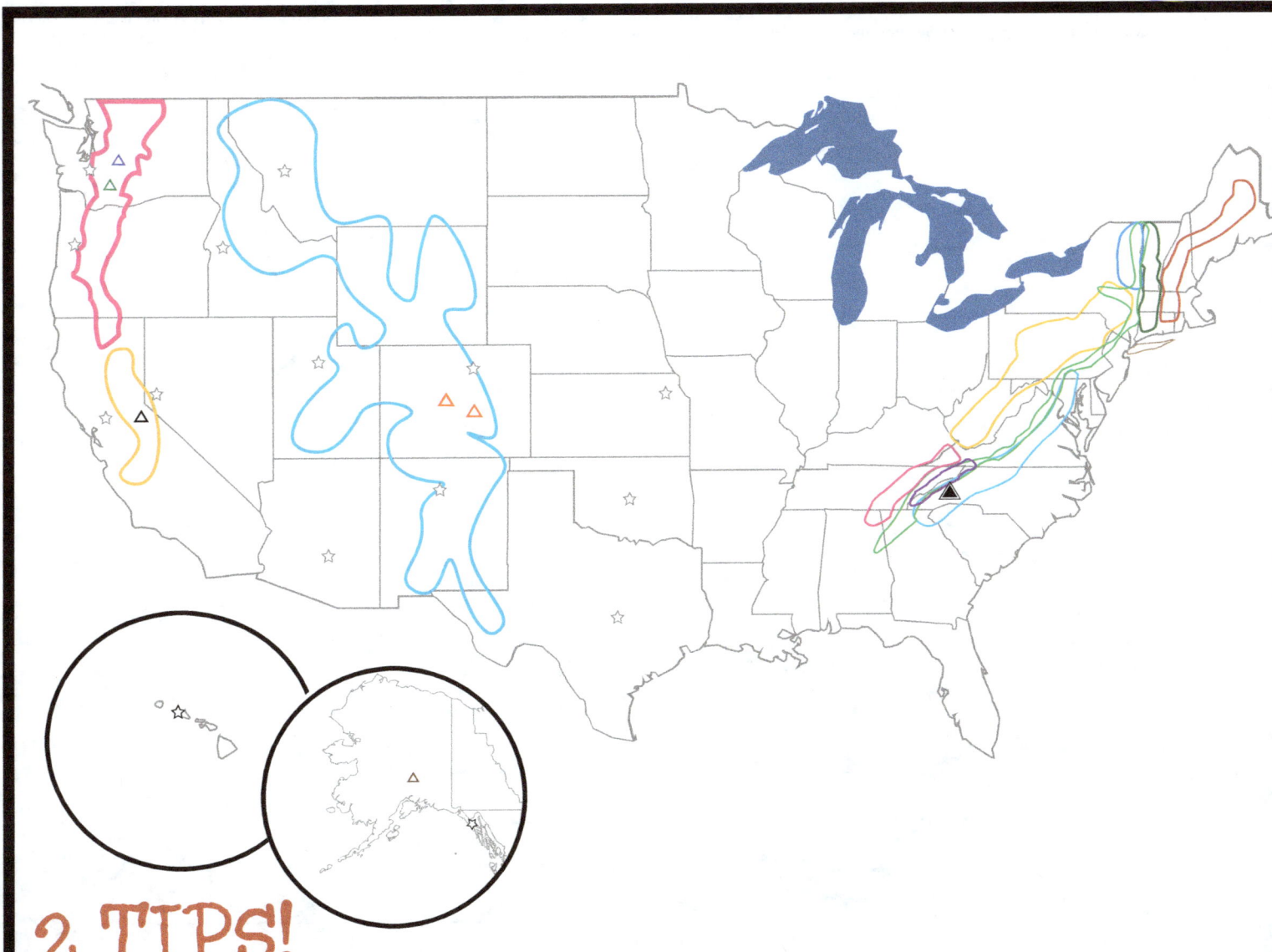

Shade & Label all geography from Lessons 8, 9, 10, 11, 12, 13, & 14:

Topeka, Kansas
Oklahoma City, Oklahoma
Austin, Texas
Denver, Colorado
Santa Fe, New Mexico

Salt Lake City, Utah
Phoenix, Arizona
Carson City, Nevada
Sacramento, California
Honolulu, Hawaii

Helena, Montana
Boise, Idaho
Olympia, Washington
Salem, Oregon
Juneau, Alaska

White Mountains
Green Mountains
Adirondack Mountains
Allegheny Mountains

The Great Valley
Blue Ridge Mountains
Great Smoky Mountains
Cumberland Mountains
Mt. Mitchell

Rocky Mountains
Pikes Peak
Mt. Elbert
Sierra Nevada
Mt. Whitney

Cascade Mountains
Mt. Rainier
Mt. St. Helens
Denali

2 TIPS!

The "Closer Look" map *(found within the Teaching & Student Resource / Tid-Bits Book)* **is a great resource when doing your TrueReview pages.** The "Closer Look" map details just the geography that you need to review for this map. **TIP #2:** Writing on maps can be hard and frustrating when there isn't enough room for the names. To fix this, take a separate sheet of paper and list the geographical names on it, giving each a number. Then, take those numbers and place them in the corresponding geographical area on this map. You can also write the geographic names in a clean space on this page and draw a clean line to the geography that the name belongs to.

TRUE REVIEW! Memorization Through Repetition

Do 2 Of This Map Per Lesson, This Map Is On The Backside Of This Page.

Week 14 REVIEW

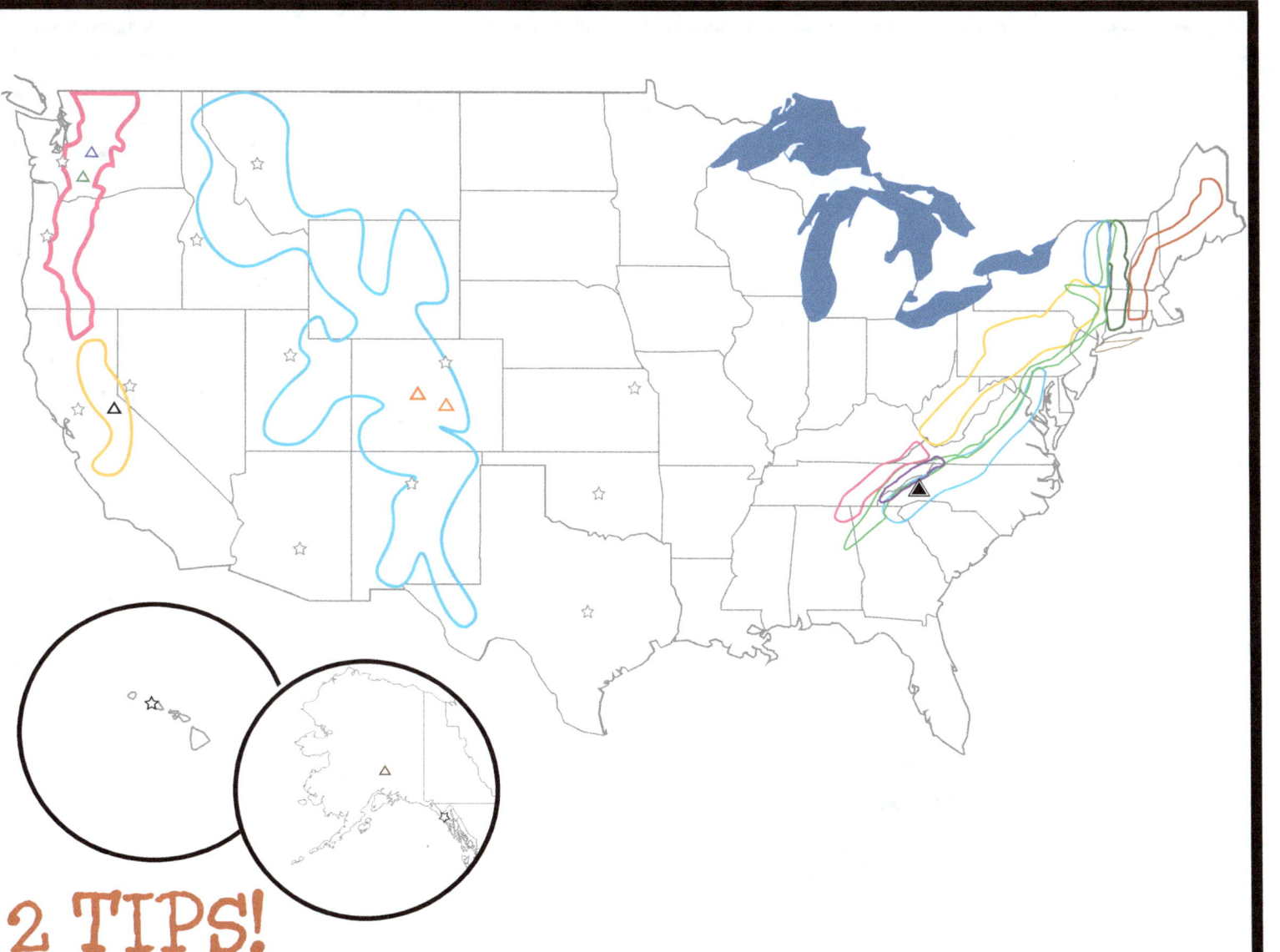

2 TIPS!

Shade & Label all geography from Lessons 8, 9, 10, 11, 12, 13, & 14:

Topeka, Kansas
Oklahoma City, Oklahoma
Austin, Texas
Denver, Colorado
Santa Fe, New Mexico

Salt Lake City, Utah
Phoenix, Arizona
Carson City, Nevada
Sacramento, California
Honolulu, Hawaii

Helena, Montana
Boise, Idaho
Olympia, Washington
Salem, Oregon
Juneau, Alaska

White Mountains
Green Mountains
Adirondack Mountains
Allegheny Mountains

The Great Valley
Blue Ridge Mountains
Great Smoky Mountains
Cumberland Mountains
Mt. Mitchell

Rocky Mountains
Pikes Peak
Mt. Elbert
Sierra Nevada
Mt. Whitney

Cascade Mountains
Mt. Rainier
Mt. St. Helens
Denali

The "Closer Look" map *(found within the Teaching & Student Resource / Tid-Bits Book)* **is a great resource when doing your TrueReview pages. The "Closer Look" map details just the geography that you need to review for this map. TIP #2:** Writing on maps can be hard and frustrating when there isn't enough room for the names. To fix this, take a separate sheet of paper and list the geographical names on it, giving each a number. Then, take those numbers and place them in the corresponding geographical area on this map. You can also write the geographic names in a clean space on this page and draw a clean line to the geography that the name belongs to.

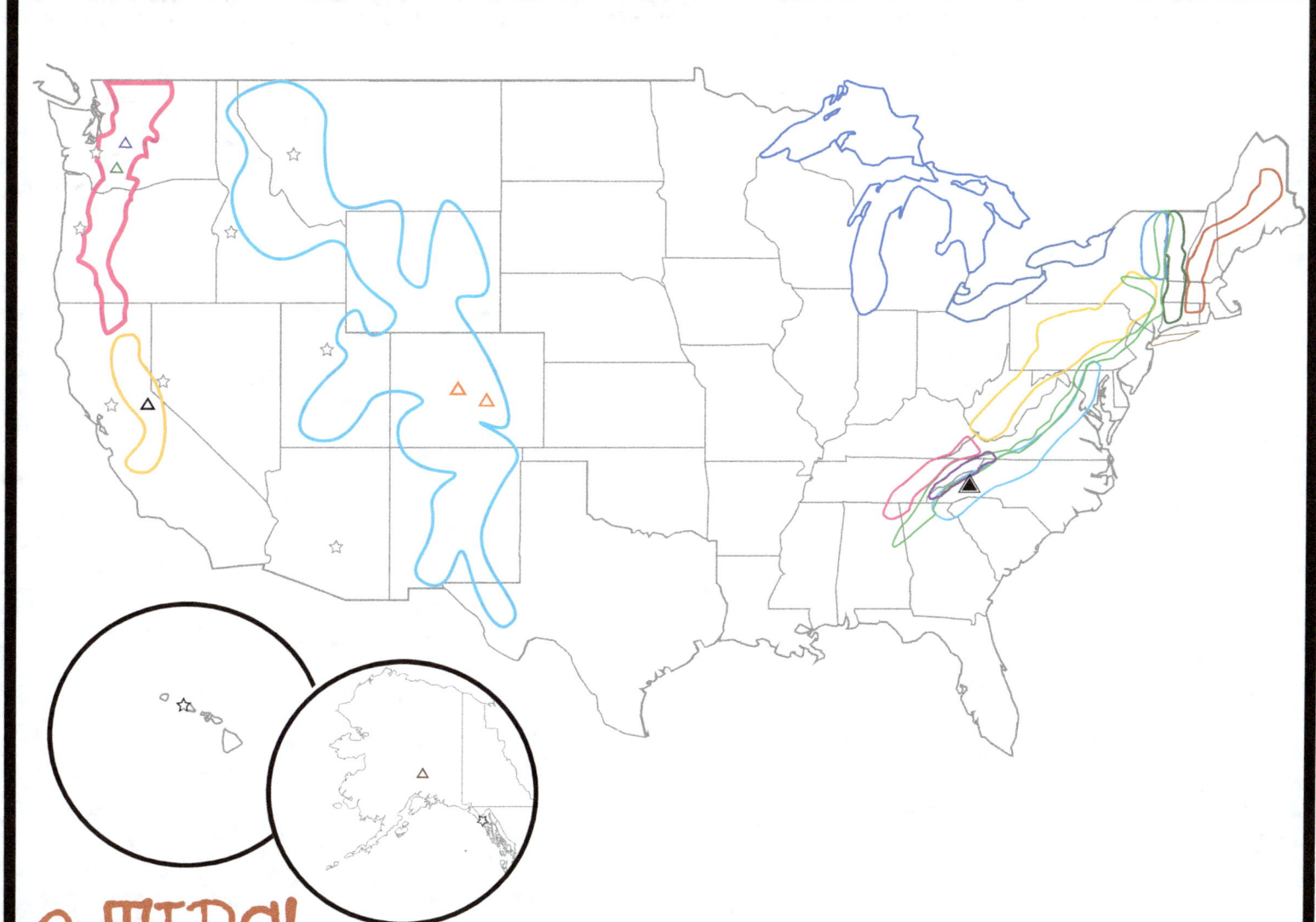

TRUE REVIEW! Memorization Through Repetition

Do 2 Of This Map Per Lesson, This Map Is On The Backside Of This Page.

Week 15 REVIEW

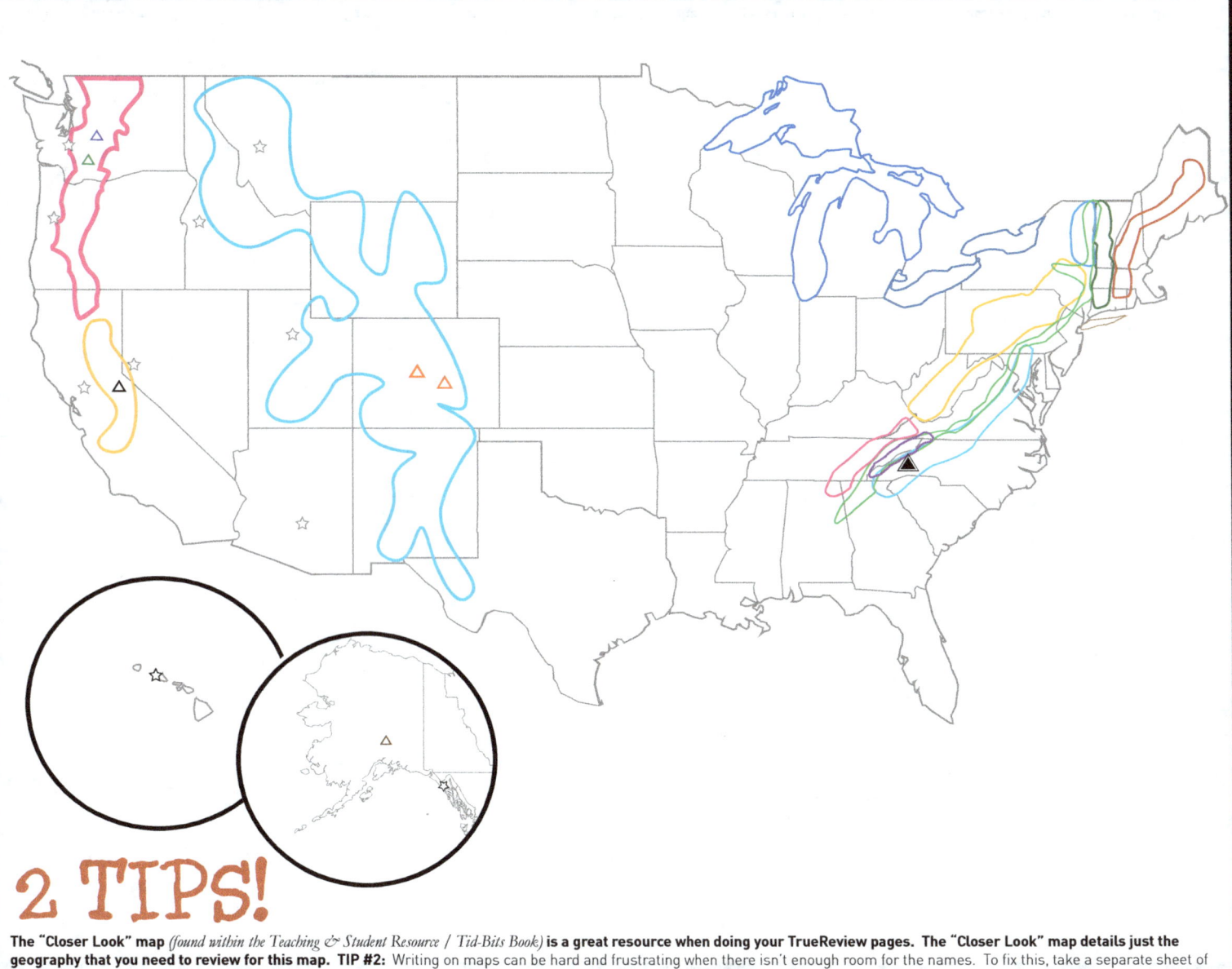

Shade & Label all geography from Lessons 9, 10, 11, 12, 13, 14, & 15:

Salt Lake City, Utah
Phoenix, Arizona
Carson City, Nevada
Sacramento, California
Honolulu, Hawaii

Helena, Montana
Boise, Idaho
Olympia, Washington
Salem, Oregon
Juneau, Alaska

White Mountains
Green Mountains
Adirondack Mountains
Allegheny Mountains

The Great Valley
Blue Ridge Mountains
Great Smoky Mountains
Cumberland Mountains
Mt. Mitchell

Rocky Mountains
Pikes Peak
Mt. Elbert
Sierra Nevada
Mt. Whitney

Cascade Mountains
Mt. Rainier
Mt. St. Helens
Denali

Lake Huron
Lake Ontario
Lake Michigan
Lake Erie
Lake Superior

2 TIPS!

The "Closer Look" map *(found within the Teaching & Student Resource / Tid-Bits Book)* **is a great resource when doing your TrueReview pages. The "Closer Look" map details just the geography that you need to review for this map. TIP #2:** Writing on maps can be hard and frustrating when there isn't enough room for the names. To fix this, take a separate sheet of paper and list the geographical names on it, giving each a number. Then, take those numbers and place them in the corresponding geographical area on this map. You can also write the geographic names in a clean space on this page and draw a clean line to the geography that the name belongs to.

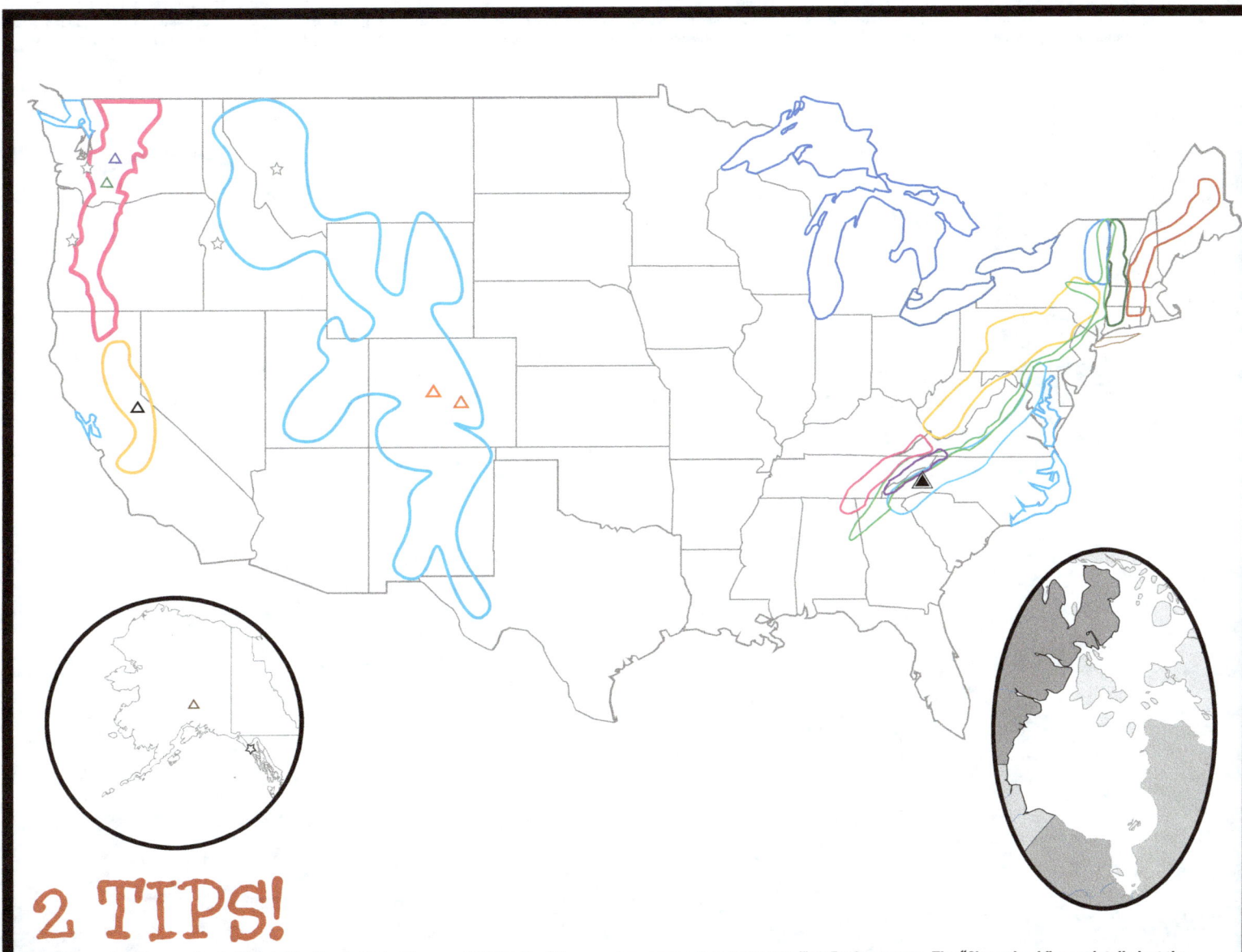

TRUE REVIEW! Memorization Through Repetition

Do 2 Of This Map Per Lesson, This Map Is On The Backside Of This Page.

Week 16 REVIEW

Shade & Label all geography from Lessons 10, 11, 12, 13, 14, 15, & 16:

Helena, Montana
Boise, Idaho
Olympia, Washington
Salem, Oregon
Juneau, Alaska

White Mountains
Green Mountains
Adirondack Mountains
Allegheny Mountains

The Great Valley
Blue Ridge Mountains
Great Smoky Mountains
Cumberland Mountains
Mt. Mitchell

Rocky Mountains
Pikes Peak
Mt. Elbert
Sierra Nevada
Mt. Whitney

Cascade Mountains
Mt. Rainier
Mt. St. Helens
Denali

Lake Huron
Lake Ontario
Lake Michigan
Lake Erie
Lake Superior

Chesapeake Bay
Hudson Bay (Canada)
San Francisco Bay
Puget Sound
Pamlico Sound

2 TIPS!

The "Closer Look" map *(found within the Teaching & Student Resource / Tid-Bits Book)* **is a great resource when doing your TrueReview pages. The "Closer Look" map details just the geography that you need to review for this map. TIP #2:** Writing on maps can be hard and frustrating when there isn't enough room for the names. To fix this, take a separate sheet of paper and list the geographical names on it, giving each a number. Then, take those numbers and place them in the corresponding geographical area on this map. You can also write the geographic names in a clean space on this page and draw a clean line to the geography that the name belongs to.

TRUE REVIEW! Memorization Through Repetition

Do 2 Of This Map Per Lesson, This Map Is On The Backside Of This Page.

Week 17 REVIEW

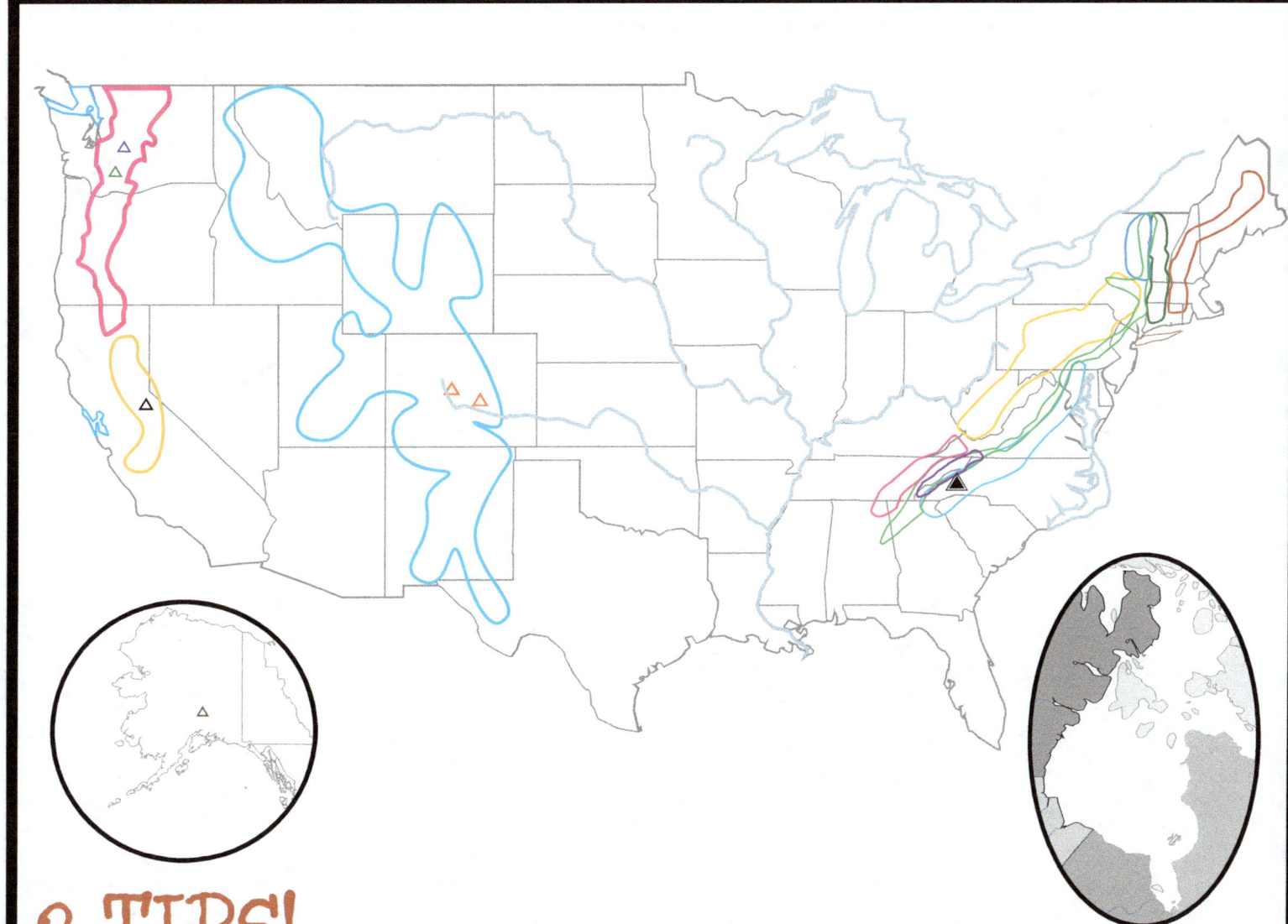

Shade & Label all geography from Lessons 11, 12, 13, 14, 15, 16, & 17:

White Mountains
Green Mountains
Adirondack Mountains
Allegheny Mountains

The Great Valley
Blue Ridge Mountains
Great Smoky Mountains
Cumberland Mountains
Mt. Mitchell

Rocky Mountains
Pikes Peak
Mt. Elbert
Sierra Nevada
Mt. Whitney

Cascade Mountains
Mt. Rainier
Mt. St. Helens
Denali

Lake Huron
Lake Ontario
Lake Michigan
Lake Erie
Lake Superior

Chesapeake Bay
Hudson Bay (Canada)
San Francisco Bay
Puget Sound
Pamlico Sound

St. Lawrence River
Ohio River
Mississippi River
Missouri River
Arkansas River

2 TIPS!

The "Closer Look" map *(found within the Teaching & Student Resource / Tid-Bits Book)* **is a great resource when doing your TrueReview pages. The "Closer Look" map details just the geography that you need to review for this map. TIP #2:** Writing on maps can be hard and frustrating when there isn't enough room for the names. To fix this, take a separate sheet of paper and list the geographical names on it, giving each a number. Then, take those numbers and place them in the corresponding geographical area on this map. You can also write the geographic names in a clean space on this page and draw a clean line to the geography that the name belongs to.

TRUE REVIEW! Memorization Through Repetition

Do 2 Of This Map Per Lesson, This Map Is On The Backside Of This Page.

Week 17 REVIEW

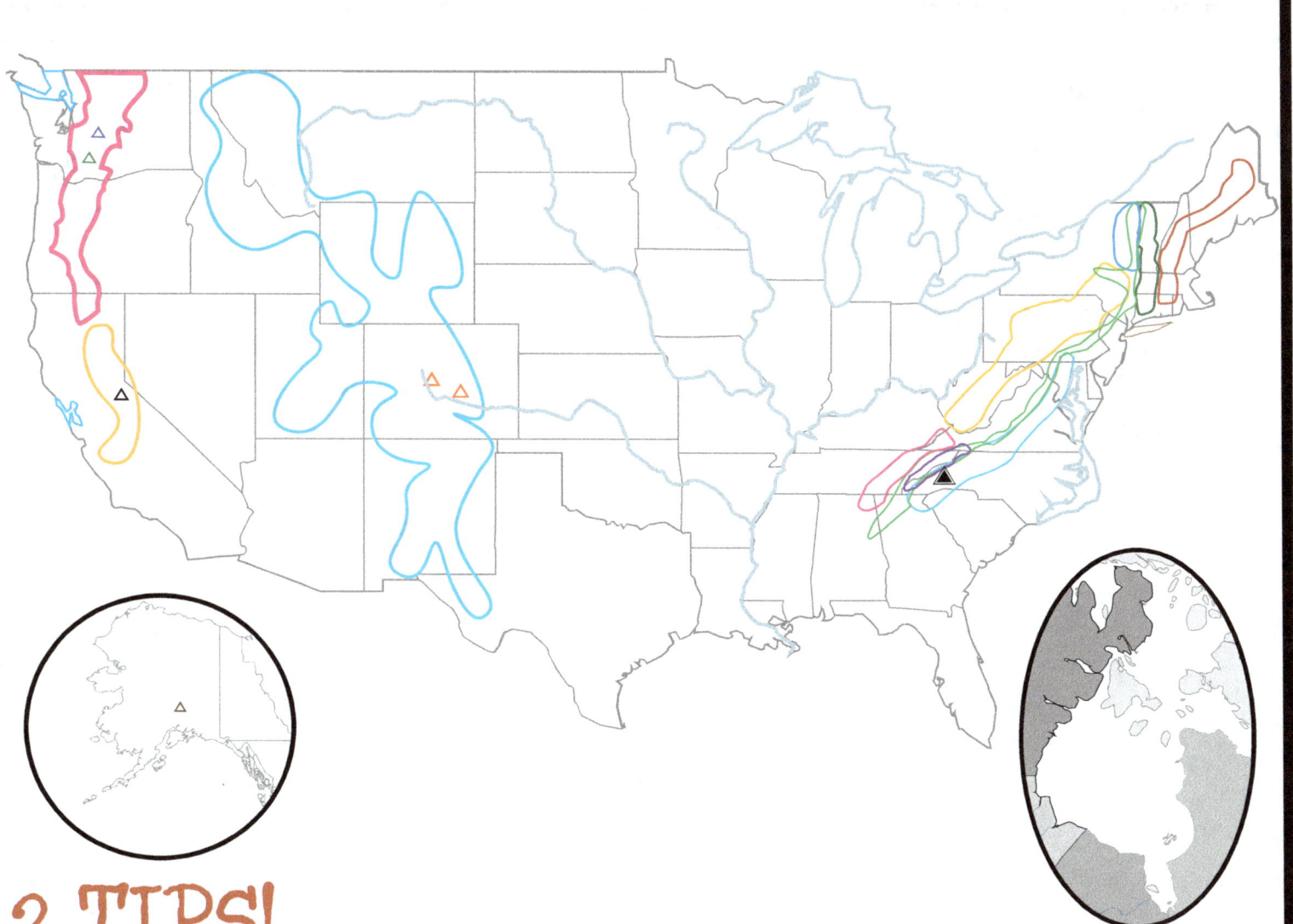

Shade & Label all geography from Lessons 11, 12, 13, 14, 15, 16, & 17:

White Mountains
Green Mountains
Adirondack Mountains
Allegheny Mountains

The Great Valley
Blue Ridge Mountains
Great Smoky Mountains
Cumberland Mountains
Mt. Mitchell

Rocky Mountains
Pikes Peak
Mt. Elbert
Sierra Nevada
Mt. Whitney

Cascade Mountains
Mt. Rainier
Mt. St. Helens
Denali

Lake Huron
Lake Ontario
Lake Michigan
Lake Erie
Lake Superior

Chesapeake Bay
Hudson Bay (Canada)
San Francisco Bay
Puget Sound
Pamlico Sound

St. Lawrence River
Ohio River
Mississippi River
Missouri River
Arkansas River

2 TIPS!

The "Closer Look" map *(found within the Teaching & Student Resource / Tid-Bits Book)* is a great resource when doing your TrueReview pages. The "Closer Look" map details just the geography that you need to review for this map. **TIP #2:** Writing on maps can be hard and frustrating when there isn't enough room for the names. To fix this, take a separate sheet of paper and list the geographical names on it, giving each a number. Then, take those numbers and place them in the corresponding geographical area on this map. You can also write the geographic names in a clean space on this page and draw a clean line to the geography that the name belongs to.

TRUE REVIEW! Memorization Through Repetition — Week 18 REVIEW

Do 2 Of This Map Per Lesson, This Map Is On The Backside Of This Page.

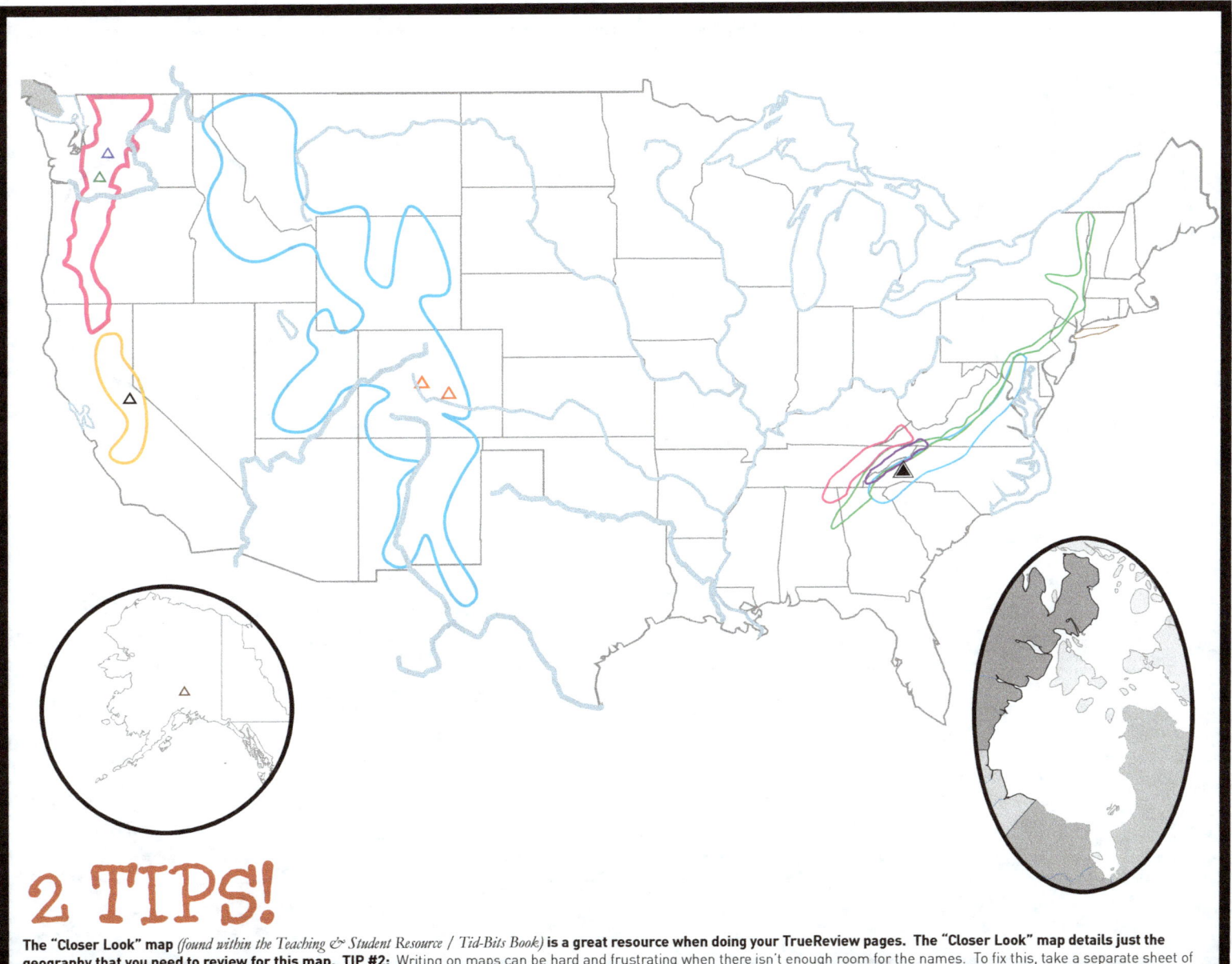

Shade & Label all geography from Lessons 12, 13, 14, 15, 16, 17, & 18:

The Great Valley
Blue Ridge Mountains
Great Smoky Mountains
Cumberland Mountains
Mt. Mitchell

Rocky Mountains
Pikes Peak
Mt. Elbert
Sierra Nevada
Mt. Whitney

Cascade Mountains
Mt. Rainier
Mt. St. Helens
Denali

Lake Huron
Lake Ontario
Lake Michigan
Lake Erie
Lake Superior

Chesapeake Bay
Hudson Bay (Canada)
San Francisco Bay
Puget Sound
Pamlico Sound

St. Lawrence River
Ohio River
Mississippi River
Missouri River
Arkansas River

Colorado River
Red River
Rio Grande River
Columbia River
Great Salt Lake

2 TIPS!

The "Closer Look" map *(found within the Teaching & Student Resource / Tid-Bits Book)* **is a great resource when doing your TrueReview pages. The "Closer Look" map details just the geography that you need to review for this map.** **TIP #2:** Writing on maps can be hard and frustrating when there isn't enough room for the names. To fix this, take a separate sheet of paper and list the geographical names on it, giving each a number. Then, take those numbers and place them in the corresponding geographical area on this map. You can also write the geographic names in a clean space on this page and draw a clean line to the geography that the name belongs to.

TRUE REVIEW! Memorization Through Repetition

Do 2 Of This Map Per Lesson, This Map Is On The Backside Of This Page.

Week 18 REVIEW

Shade & Label all geography from Lessons 12, 13, 14, 15, 16, 17, & 18:

The Great Valley
Blue Ridge Mountains
Great Smoky Mountains
Cumberland Mountains
Mt. Mitchell

Rocky Mountains
Pikes Peak
Mt. Elbert
Sierra Nevada
Mt. Whitney

Cascade Mountains
Mt. Rainier
Mt. St. Helens
Denali

Lake Huron
Lake Ontario
Lake Michigan
Lake Erie
Lake Superior

Chesapeake Bay
Hudson Bay (Canada)
San Francisco Bay
Puget Sound
Pamlico Sound

St. Lawrence River
Ohio River
Mississippi River
Missouri River
Arkansas River

Colorado River
Red River
Rio Grande River
Columbia River
Great Salt Lake

2 TIPS!

The **"Closer Look" map** *(found within the Teaching & Student Resource / Tid-Bits Book)* **is a great resource when doing your TrueReview pages. The "Closer Look" map details just the geography that you need to review for this map. TIP #2:** Writing on maps can be hard and frustrating when there isn't enough room for the names. To fix this, take a separate sheet of paper and list the geographical names on it, giving each a number. Then, take those numbers and place them in the corresponding geographical area on this map. You can also write the geographic names in a clean space on this page and draw a clean line to the geography that the name belongs to.

TRUE REVIEW! Memorization Through Repetition

Do 2 Of This Map Per Lesson, This Map Is On The Backside Of This Page.

Week 19 REVIEW

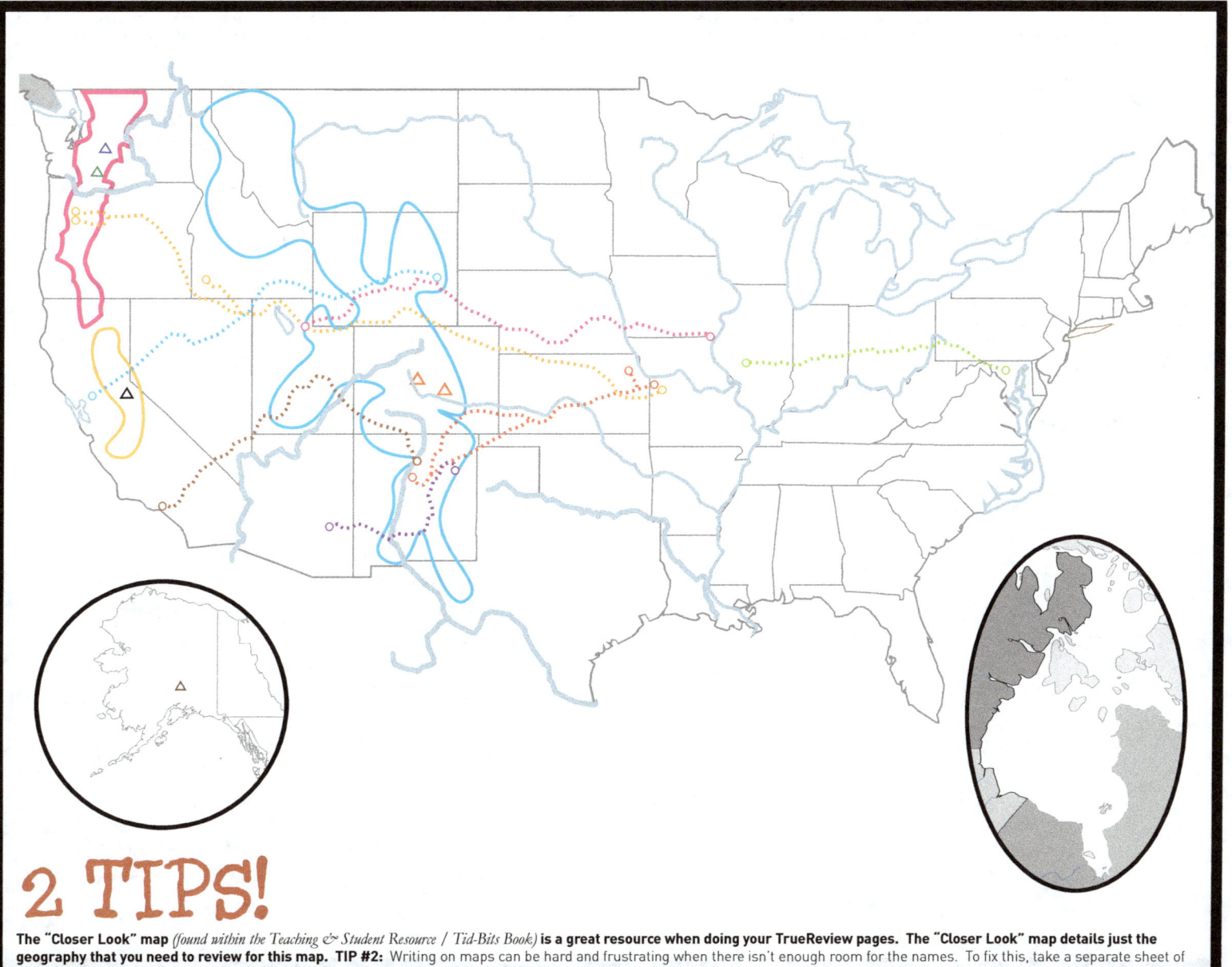

Shade & Label all geography from Lessons 13, 14, 15, 16, 17, 18, & 19:

Rocky Mountains
Pikes Peak
Mt. Elbert
Sierra Nevada
Mt. Whitney

Cascade Mountains
Mt. Rainier
Mt. St. Helens
Denali

Lake Huron
Lake Ontario
Lake Michigan
Lake Erie
Lake Superior

Chesapeake Bay
Hudson Bay (Canada)
San Francisco Bay
Puget Sound
Pamlico Sound

St. Lawrence River
Ohio River
Mississippi River
Missouri River
Arkansas River

Colorado River
Red River
Rio Grande River
Columbia River
Great Salt Lake

Cumberland Road
Santa Fe Trail
Mormon Trail
Gila Trail
Old Spanish Trail
California Trail
Oregon Trail

2 TIPS!

The "Closer Look" map *(found within the Teaching & Student Resource / Tid-Bits Book)* **is a great resource when doing your TrueReview pages. The "Closer Look" map details just the geography that you need to review for this map. TIP #2:** Writing on maps can be hard and frustrating when there isn't enough room for the names. To fix this, take a separate sheet of paper and list the geographical names on it, giving each a number. Then, take those numbers and place them in the corresponding geographical area on this map. You can also write the geographic names in a clean space on this page and draw a clean line to the geography that the name belongs to.

TRUE REVIEW! Memorization Through Repetition

Do 2 Of This Map Per Lesson, This Map Is On The Backside Of This Page.

Week 19 REVIEW

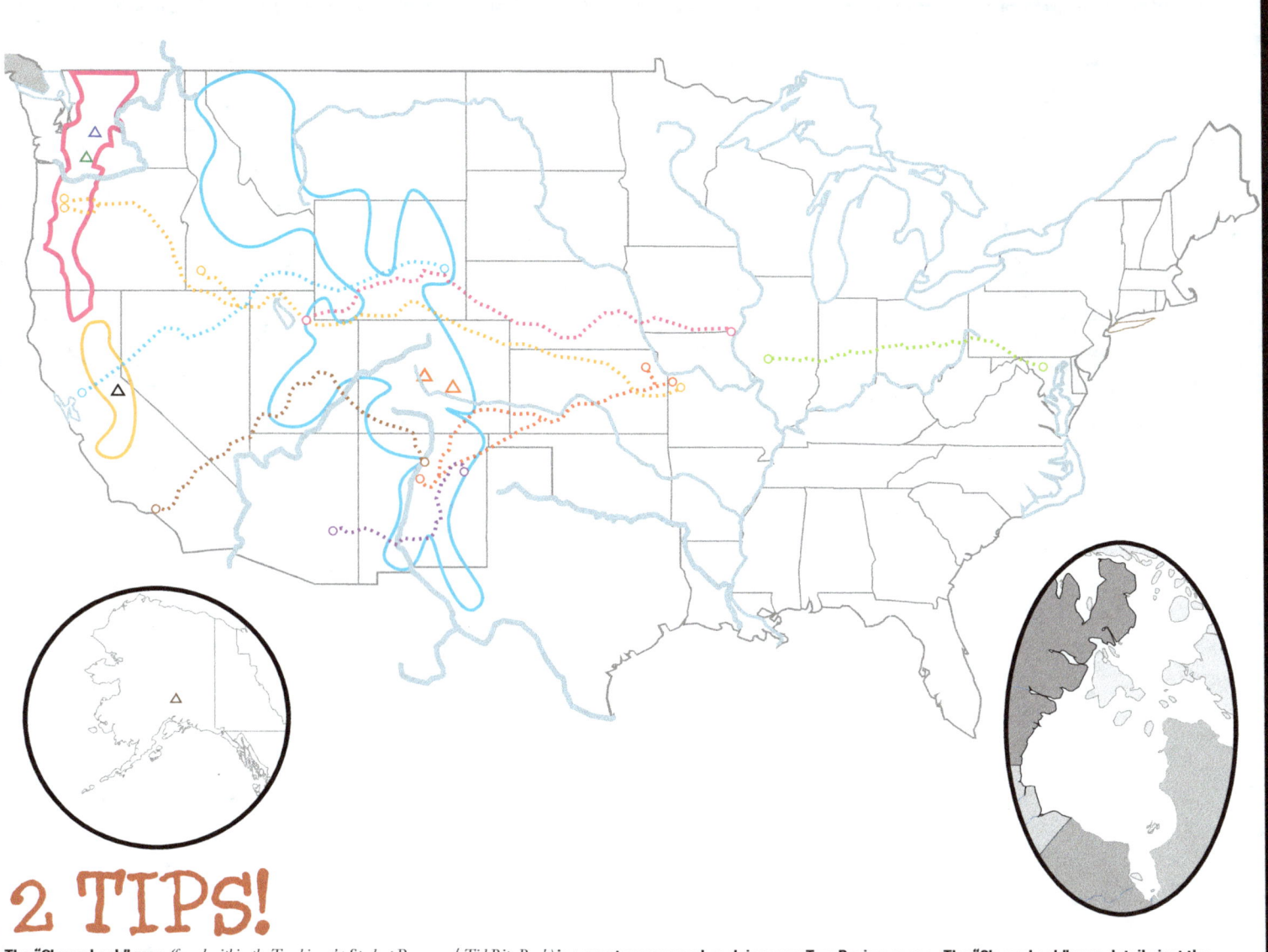

2 TIPS!

The "Closer Look" map *(found within the Teaching & Student Resource / Tid-Bits Book)* **is a great resource when doing your TrueReview pages. The "Closer Look" map details just the geography that you need to review for this map. TIP #2:** Writing on maps can be hard and frustrating when there isn't enough room for the names. To fix this, take a separate sheet of paper and list the geographical names on it, giving each a number. Then, take those numbers and place them in the corresponding geographical area on this map. You can also write the geographic names in a clean space on this page and draw a clean line to the geography that the name belongs to.

Shade & Label all geography from Lessons 13, 14, 15, 16, 17, 18, & 19:

Rocky Mountains
Pikes Peak
Mt. Elbert
Sierra Nevada
Mt. Whitney

Cascade Mountains
Mt. Rainier
Mt. St. Helens
Denali

Lake Huron
Lake Ontario
Lake Michigan
Lake Erie
Lake Superior

Chesapeake Bay
Hudson Bay (Canada)
San Francisco Bay
Puget Sound
Pamlico Sound

St. Lawrence River
Ohio River
Mississippi River
Missouri River
Arkansas River

Colorado River
Red River
Rio Grande River
Columbia River
Great Salt Lake

Cumberland Road
Santa Fe Trail
Mormon Trail
Gila Trail
Old Spanish Trail
California Trail
Oregon Trail

TRUE REVIEW! Memorization Through Repetition

Do 2 Of This Map Per Lesson, This Map Is On The Backside Of This Page.

Week 20 REVIEW

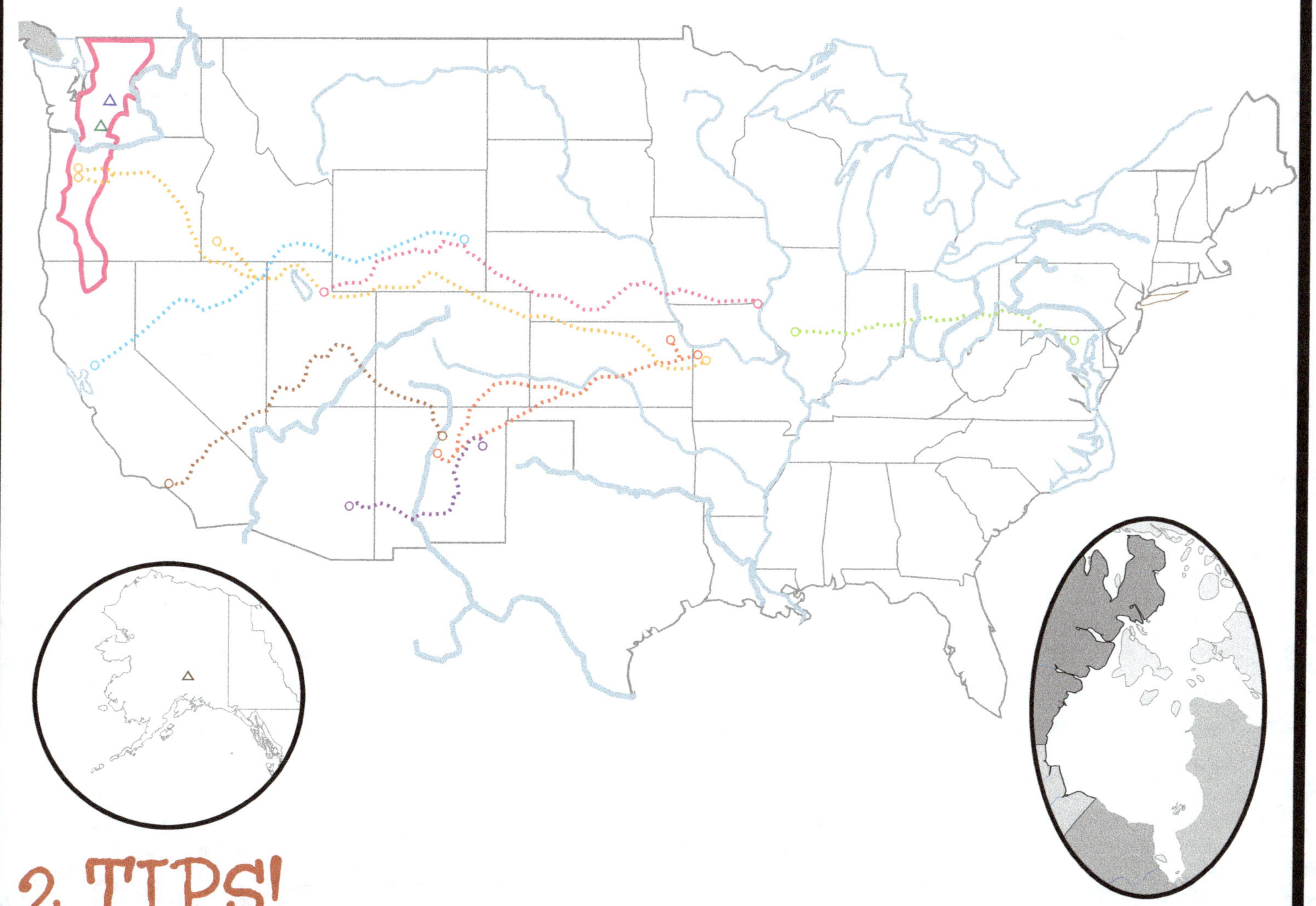

Shade & Label all geography from Lessons 14, 15, 16, 17, 18, 19, & 20:

Cascade Mountains
Mt. Rainier
Mt. St. Helens
Denali

Lake Huron
Lake Ontario
Lake Michigan
Lake Erie
Lake Superior

Chesapeake Bay
Hudson Bay (Canada)
San Francisco Bay
Puget Sound
Pamlico Sound

St. Lawrence River
Ohio River
Mississippi River
Missouri River
Arkansas River

Colorado River
Red River
Rio Grande River
Columbia River
Great Salt Lake

Cumberland Road
Santa Fe Trail
Mormon Trail
Gila Trail
Old Spanish Trail
California Trail
Oregon Trail

Erie Canal
Pennsylvania Canal
Chesapeake & Ohio Canal
Ohio & Erie Canal
Miami & Erie Canal

2 TIPS!

The "Closer Look" map *(found within the Teaching & Student Resource / Tid-Bits Book)* **is a great resource when doing your TrueReview pages. The "Closer Look" map details just the geography that you need to review for this map. TIP #2:** Writing on maps can be hard and frustrating when there isn't enough room for the names. To fix this, take a separate sheet of paper and list the geographical names on it, giving each a number. Then, take those numbers and place them in the corresponding geographical area on this map. You can also write the geographic names in a clean space on this page and draw a clean line to the geography that the name belongs to.

89

TRUE REVIEW! Memorization Through Repetition

Do 2 Of This Map Per Lesson, This Map Is On The Backside Of This Page.

Week 20 REVIEW

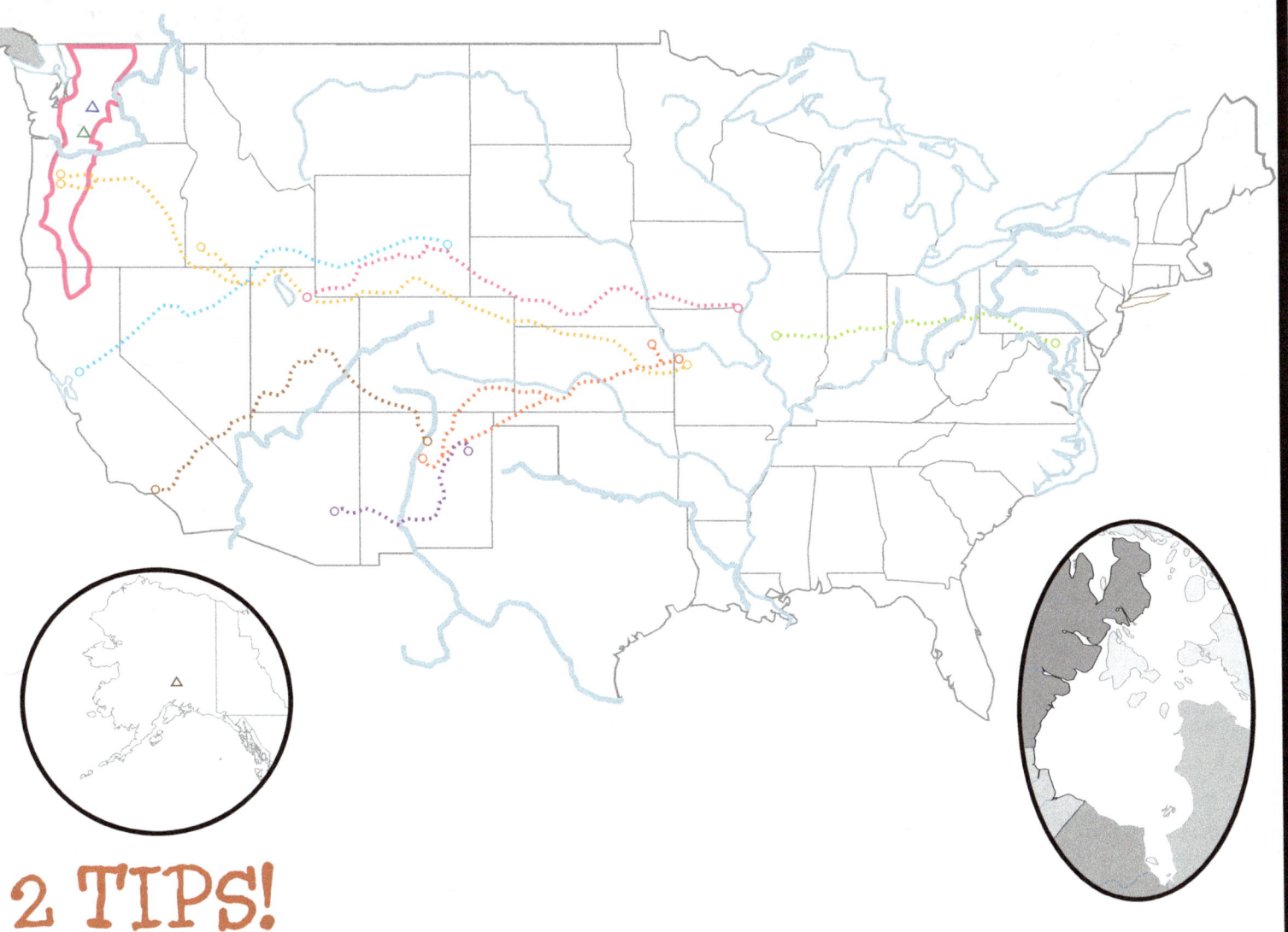

Shade & Label all geography from Lessons 14, 15, 16, 17, 18, 19, & 20:

Cascade Mountains
Mt. Rainier
Mt. St. Helens
Denali

Lake Huron
Lake Ontario
Lake Michigan
Lake Erie
Lake Superior

Chesapeake Bay
Hudson Bay (Canada)
San Francisco Bay
Puget Sound
Pamlico Sound

St. Lawrence River
Ohio River
Mississippi River
Missouri River
Arkansas River

Colorado River
Red River
Rio Grande River
Columbia River
Great Salt Lake

Cumberland Road
Santa Fe Trail
Mormon Trail
Gila Trail
Old Spanish Trail
California Trail
Oregon Trail

Erie Canal
Pennsylvania Canal
Chesapeake & Ohio Canal
Ohio & Erie Canal
Miami & Erie Canal

2 TIPS!

The "Closer Look" map *(found within the Teaching & Student Resource / Tid-Bits Book)* **is a great resource when doing your TrueReview pages. The "Closer Look" map details just the geography that you need to review for this map. TIP #2:** Writing on maps can be hard and frustrating when there isn't enough room for the names. To fix this, take a separate sheet of paper and list the geographical names on it, giving each a number. Then, take those numbers and place them in the corresponding geographical area on this map. You can also write the geographic names in a clean space on this page and draw a clean line to the geography that the name belongs to.

TRUE REVIEW! Memorization Through Repetition

Do 2 Of This Map Per Lesson, This Map Is On The Backside Of This Page.

Week 21 REVIEW

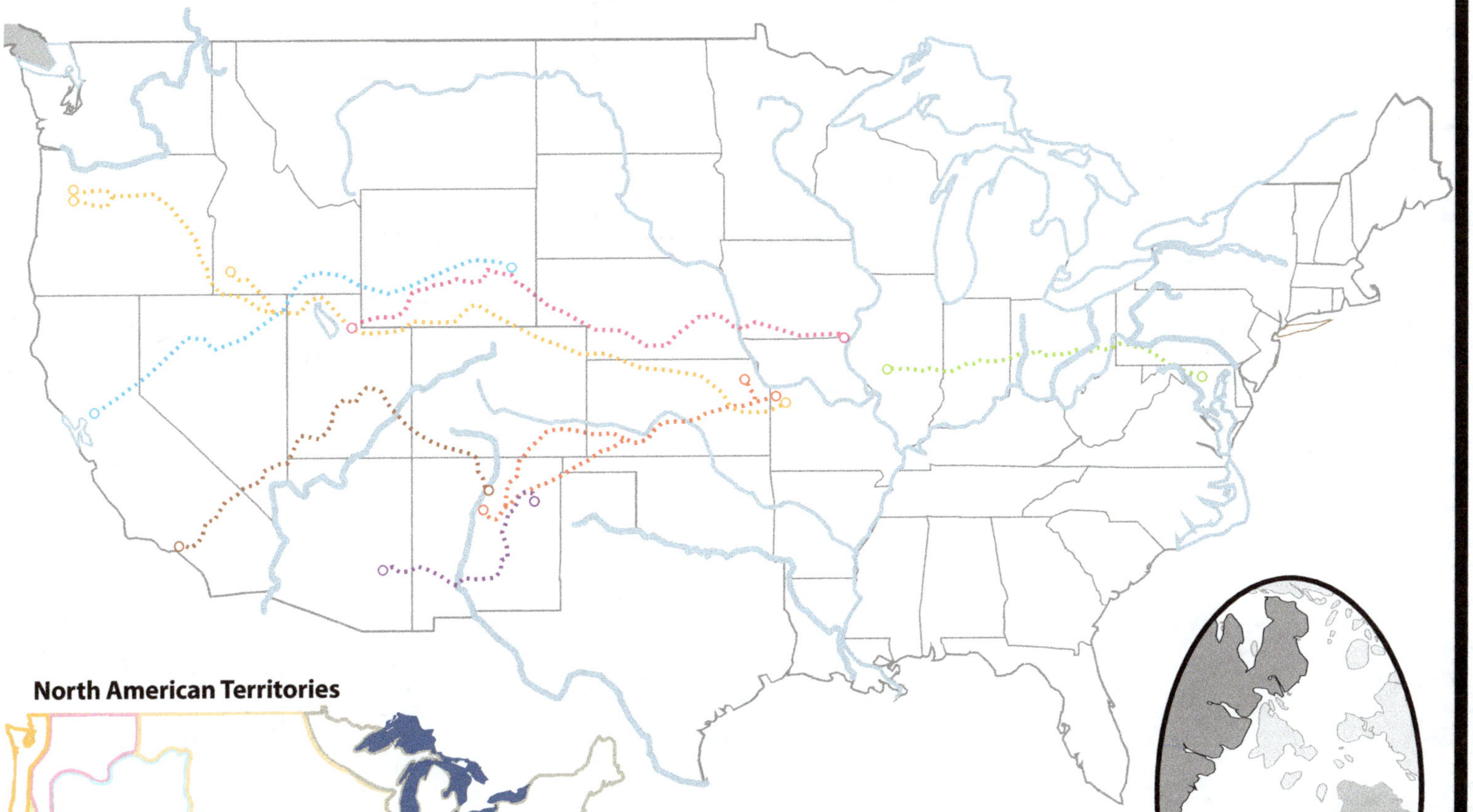

Shade & Label all geography from Lessons 15, 16, 17, 18, 19, 20, & 21:

Lake Huron
Lake Ontario
Lake Michigan
Lake Erie
Lake Superior

Chesapeake Bay
Hudson Bay (Canada)
San Francisco Bay
Puget Sound
Pamlico Sound

St. Lawrence River
Ohio River
Mississippi River
Missouri River
Arkansas River

Colorado River
Red River
Rio Grande River
Columbia River
Great Salt Lake

Cumberland Road
Santa Fe Trail
Mormon Trail
Gila Trail
Old Spanish Trail
California Trail
Oregon Trail

Erie Canal
Pennsylvania Canal
Chesapeake & Ohio Canal
Ohio & Erie Canal
Miami & Erie Canal

Eastern Woodlands
Plains
Plateau
Northwest Coast
California
Great Basin
Southwest

North American Territories

2 TIPS!

The "Closer Look" map *(found within the Teaching & Student Resource / Tid-Bits Book)* **is a great resource when doing your TrueReview pages.** The "Closer Look" map details just the geography that you need to review for this map. **TIP #2:** Writing on maps can be hard and frustrating when there isn't enough room for the names. To fix this, take a separate sheet of paper and list the geographical names on it, giving each a number. Then, take those numbers and place them in the corresponding geographical area on this map. You can also write the geographic names in a clean space on this page and draw a clean line to the geography that the name belongs to.

TRUE REVIEW! Memorization Through Repetition

Do 2 Of This Map Per Lesson, This Map Is On The Backside Of This Page.

Week 21 REVIEW

Shade & Label all geography from Lessons 15, 16, 17, 18, 19, 20, & 21:

Lake Huron
Lake Ontario
Lake Michigan
Lake Erie
Lake Superior

Chesapeake Bay
Hudson Bay (Canada)
San Francisco Bay
Puget Sound
Pamlico Sound

St. Lawrence River
Ohio River
Mississippi River
Missouri River
Arkansas River

Colorado River
Red River
Rio Grande River
Columbia River
Great Salt Lake

Cumberland Road
Santa Fe Trail
Mormon Trail
Gila Trail
Old Spanish Trail
California Trail
Oregon Trail

Erie Canal
Pennsylvania Canal
Chesapeake & Ohio Canal
Ohio & Erie Canal
Miami & Erie Canal

Eastern Woodlands
Plains
Plateau
Northwest Coast
California
Great Basin
Southwest

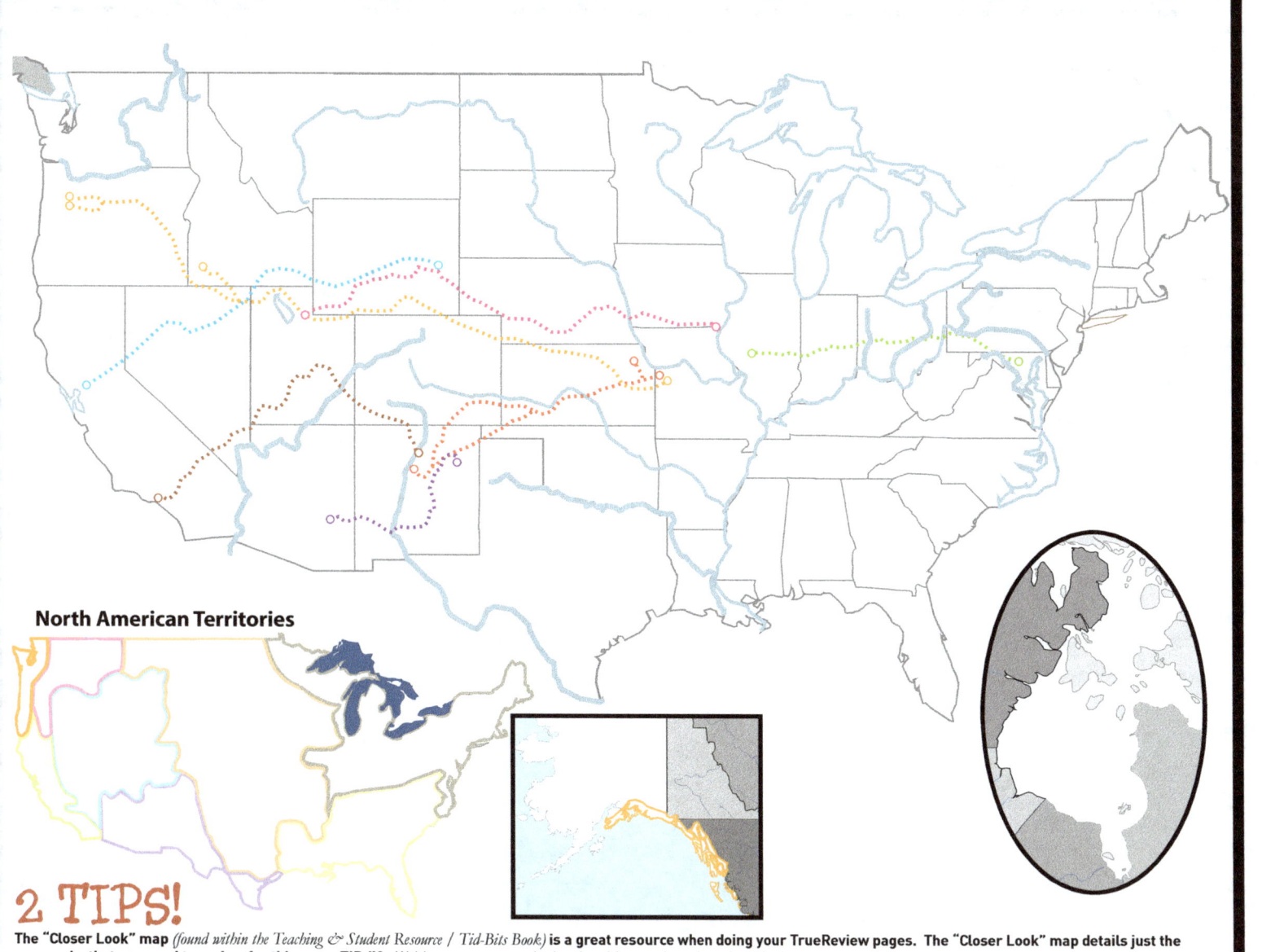

North American Territories

2 TIPS!

The "Closer Look" map *(found within the Teaching & Student Resource / Tid-Bits Book)* **is a great resource when doing your TrueReview pages. The "Closer Look" map details just the geography that you need to review for this map. TIP #2:** Writing on maps can be hard and frustrating when there isn't enough room for the names. To fix this, take a separate sheet of paper and list the geographical names on it, giving each a number. Then, take those numbers and place them in the corresponding geographical area on this map. You can also write the geographic names in a clean space on this page and draw a clean line to the geography that the name belongs to.

TRUE REVIEW! Memorization Through Repetition — Week 22 REVIEW

Do 2 Of This Map Per Lesson, This Map Is On The Backside Of This Page.

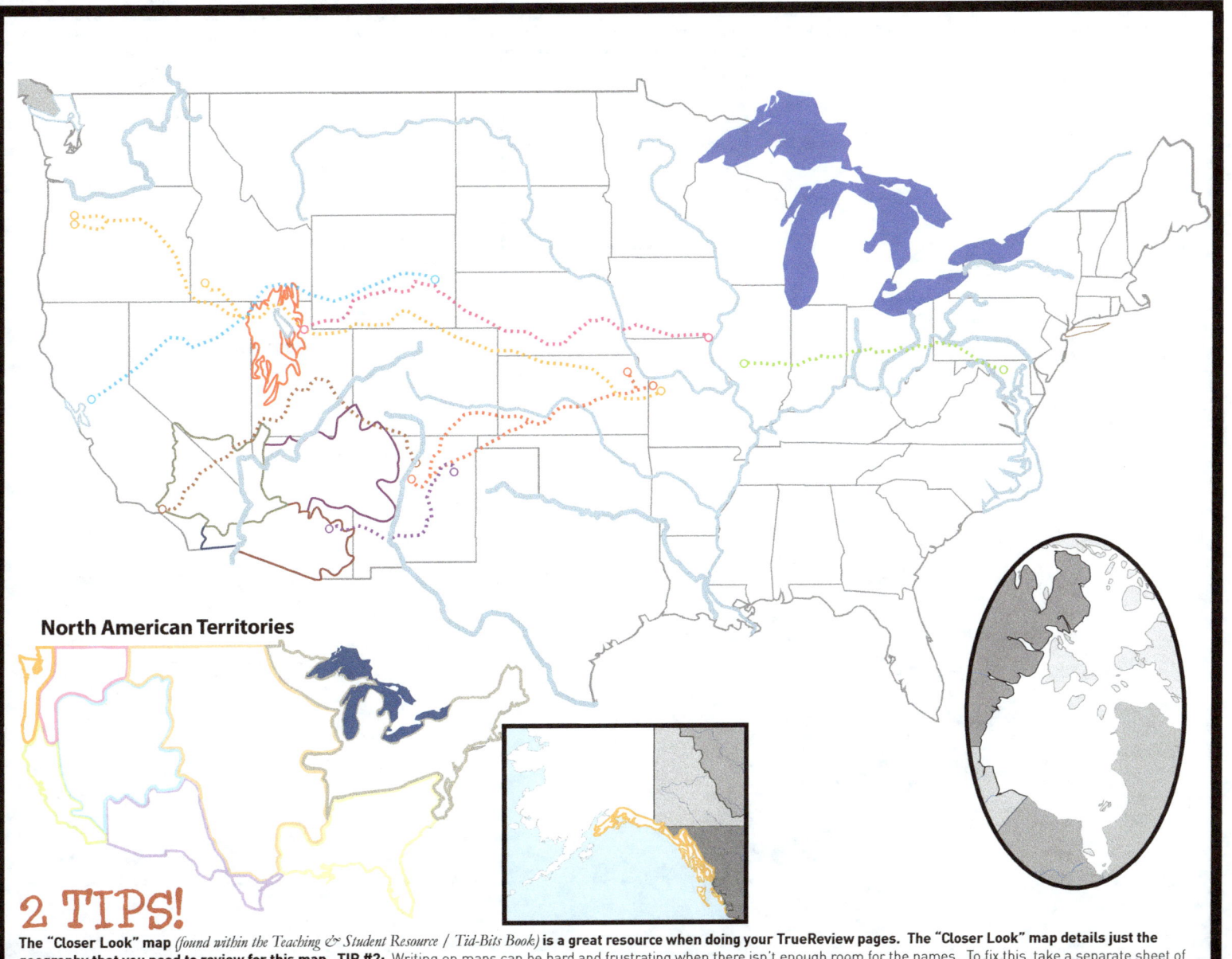

Shade & Label all geography from Lessons 16, 17, 18, 19, 20, 21, & 22:

Chesapeake Bay
Hudson Bay (Canada)
San Francisco Bay
Puget Sound
Pamlico Sound

St. Lawrence River
Ohio River
Mississippi River
Missouri River
Arkansas River

Colorado River
Red River
Rio Grande River
Columbia River
Great Salt Lake

Cumberland Road
Santa Fe Trail
Mormon Trail
Gila Trail
Old Spanish Trail
California Trail
Oregon Trail

Erie Canal
Pennsylvania Canal
Chesapeake & Ohio Canal
Ohio & Erie Canal
Miami & Erie Canal

Eastern Woodlands
Plains
Plateau
Northwest Coast
California
Great Basin
Southwest

Mojave Desert
Sonoran Desert
Colorado Desert
Painted Desert
Great Salt Lake Desert

2 TIPS!

The "Closer Look" map *(found within the Teaching & Student Resource / Tid-Bits Book)* **is a great resource when doing your TrueReview pages. The "Closer Look" map details just the geography that you need to review for this map. TIP #2:** Writing on maps can be hard and frustrating when there isn't enough room for the names. To fix this, take a separate sheet of paper and list the geographical names on it, giving each a number. Then, take those numbers and place them in the corresponding geographical area on this map. You can also write the geographic names in a clean space on this page and draw a clean line to the geography that the name belongs to.

TRUE REVIEW! Memorization Through Repetition

Do 2 Of This Map Per Lesson, This Map Is On The Backside Of This Page.

Week 22 REVIEW

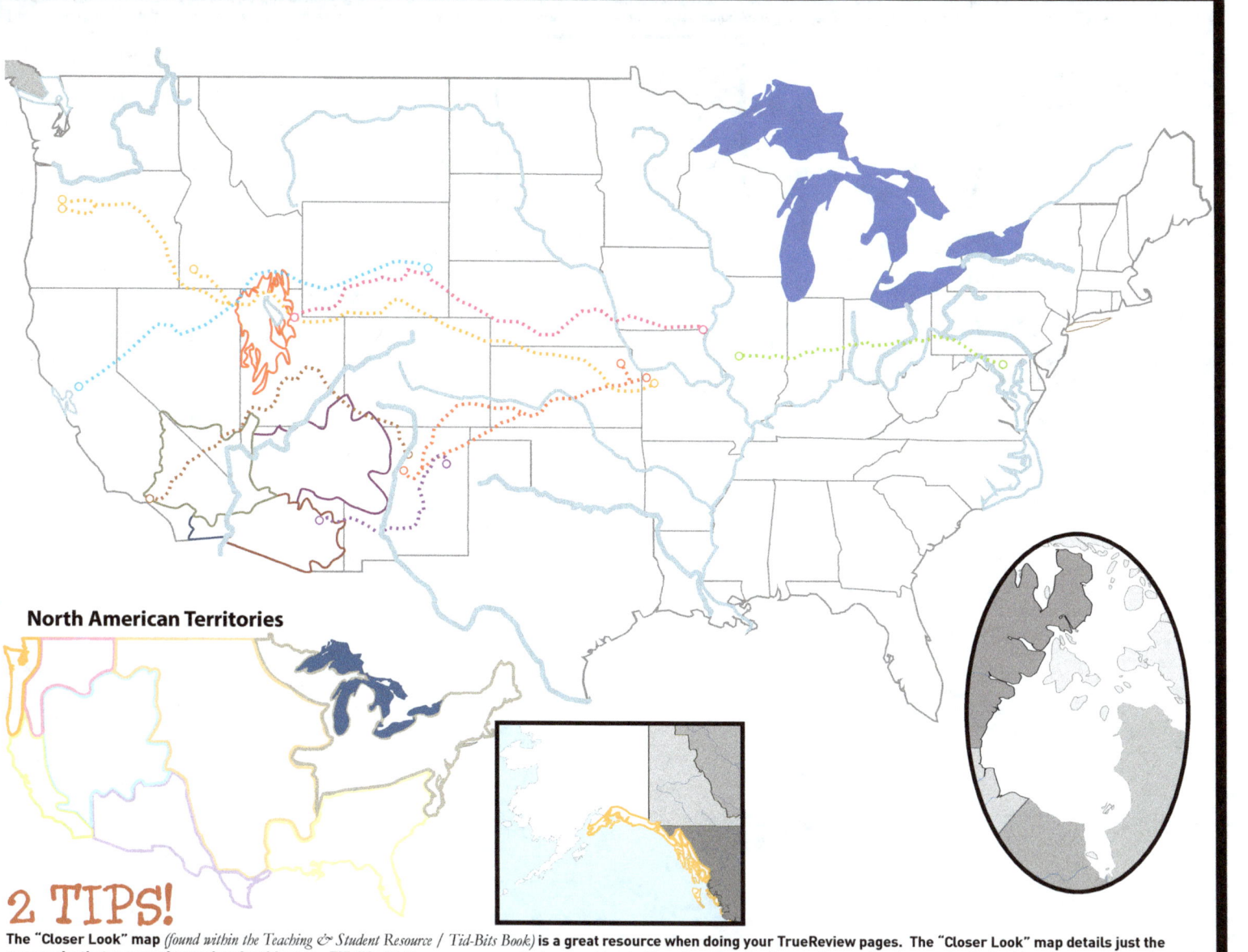

North American Territories

2 TIPS!

The "Closer Look" map *(found within the Teaching & Student Resource / Tid-Bits Book)* **is a great resource when doing your TrueReview pages. The "Closer Look" map details just the geography that you need to review for this map. TIP #2:** Writing on maps can be hard and frustrating when there isn't enough room for the names. To fix this, take a separate sheet of paper and list the geographical names on it, giving each a number. Then, take those numbers and place them in the corresponding geographical area on this map. You can also write the geographic names in a clean space on this page and draw a clean line to the geography that the name belongs to.

Shade & Label all geography from Lessons 16, 17, 18, 19, 20, 21, & 22:

Chesapeake Bay
Hudson Bay (Canada)
San Francisco Bay
Puget Sound
Pamlico Sound

St. Lawrence River
Ohio River
Mississippi River
Missouri River
Arkansas River

Colorado River
Red River
Rio Grande River
Columbia River
Great Salt Lake

Cumberland Road
Santa Fe Trail
Mormon Trail
Gila Trail
Old Spanish Trail
California Trail
Oregon Trail

Erie Canal
Pennsylvania Canal
Chesapeake & Ohio Canal
Ohio & Erie Canal
Miami & Erie Canal

Eastern Woodlands
Plains
Plateau
Northwest Coast
California
Great Basin
Southwest

Mojave Desert
Sonoran Desert
Colorado Desert
Painted Desert
Great Salt Lake Desert

TRUE REVIEW! Memorization Through Repetition

Do 2 Of This Map Per Lesson, This Map Is On The Backside Of This Page.

Week 23 REVIEW

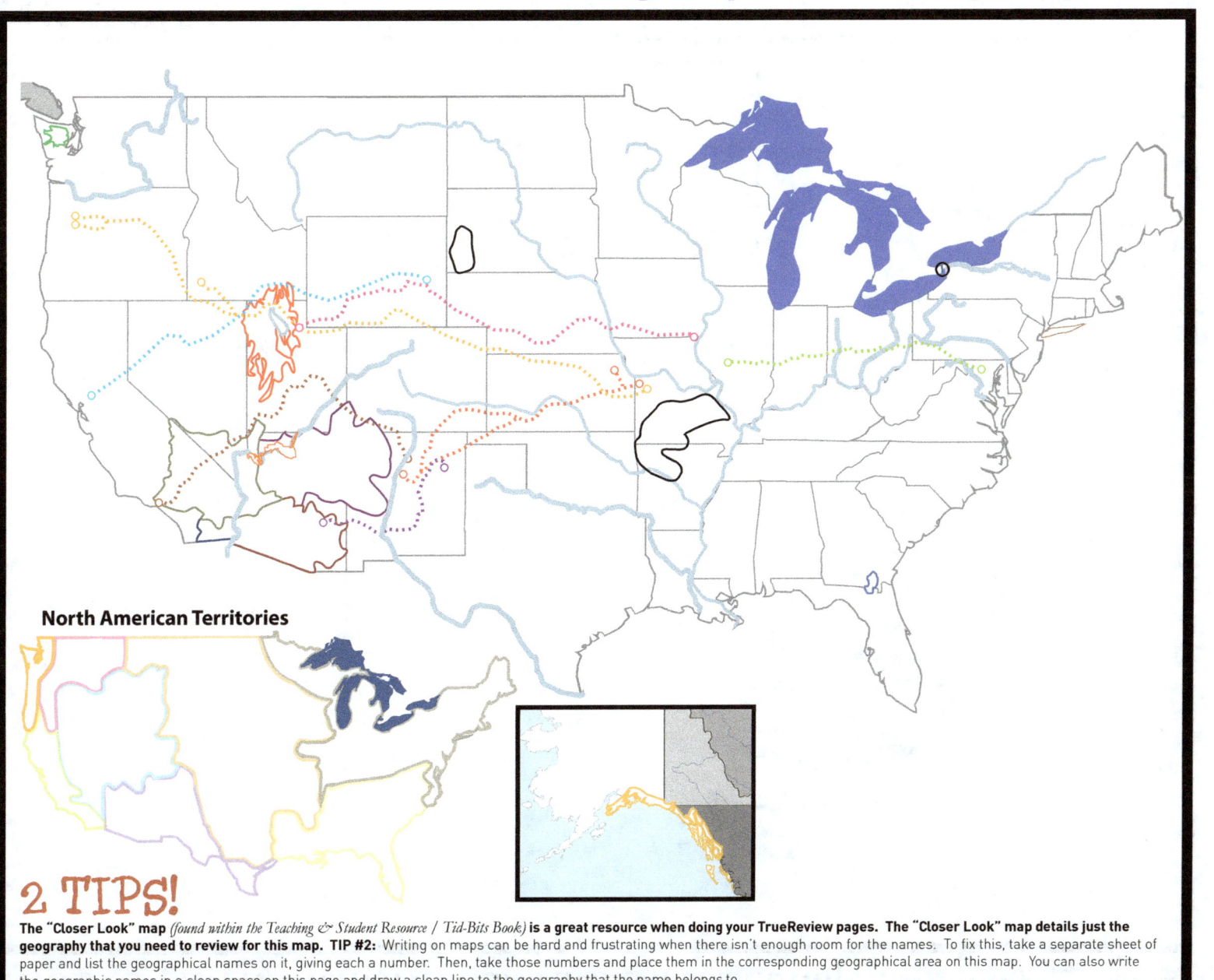

Shade & Label all geography from Lessons 17, 18, 19, 20, 21, 22, & 23:

St. Lawrence River
Ohio River
Mississippi River
Missouri River
Arkansas River

Colorado River
Red River
Rio Grande River
Columbia River
Great Salt Lake

Cumberland Road
Santa Fe Trail
Mormon Trail
Gila Trail
Old Spanish Trail
California Trail
Oregon Trail

Erie Canal
Pennsylvania Canal
Chesapeake & Ohio Canal
Ohio & Erie Canal
Miami & Erie Canal

Eastern Woodlands
Plains
Plateau
Northwest Coast
California
Great Basin
Southwest

Mojave Desert
Sonoran Desert
Colorado Desert
Painted Desert
Great Salt Lake Desert

Grand Canyon
Black Hills
Ozark Highlands
Okefenokee Swamp
Olympic Rainforests
Niagara Falls

2 TIPS!

The "Closer Look" map *(found within the Teaching & Student Resource / Tid-Bits Book)* **is a great resource when doing your TrueReview pages. The "Closer Look" map details just the geography that you need to review for this map. TIP #2:** Writing on maps can be hard and frustrating when there isn't enough room for the names. To fix this, take a separate sheet of paper and list the geographical names on it, giving each a number. Then, take those numbers and place them in the corresponding geographical area on this map. You can also write the geographic names in a clean space on this page and draw a clean line to the geography that the name belongs to.

TRUE REVIEW! Memorization Through Repetition

Do 2 Of This Map Per Lesson, This Map Is On The Backside Of This Page.

Week 23 REVIEW

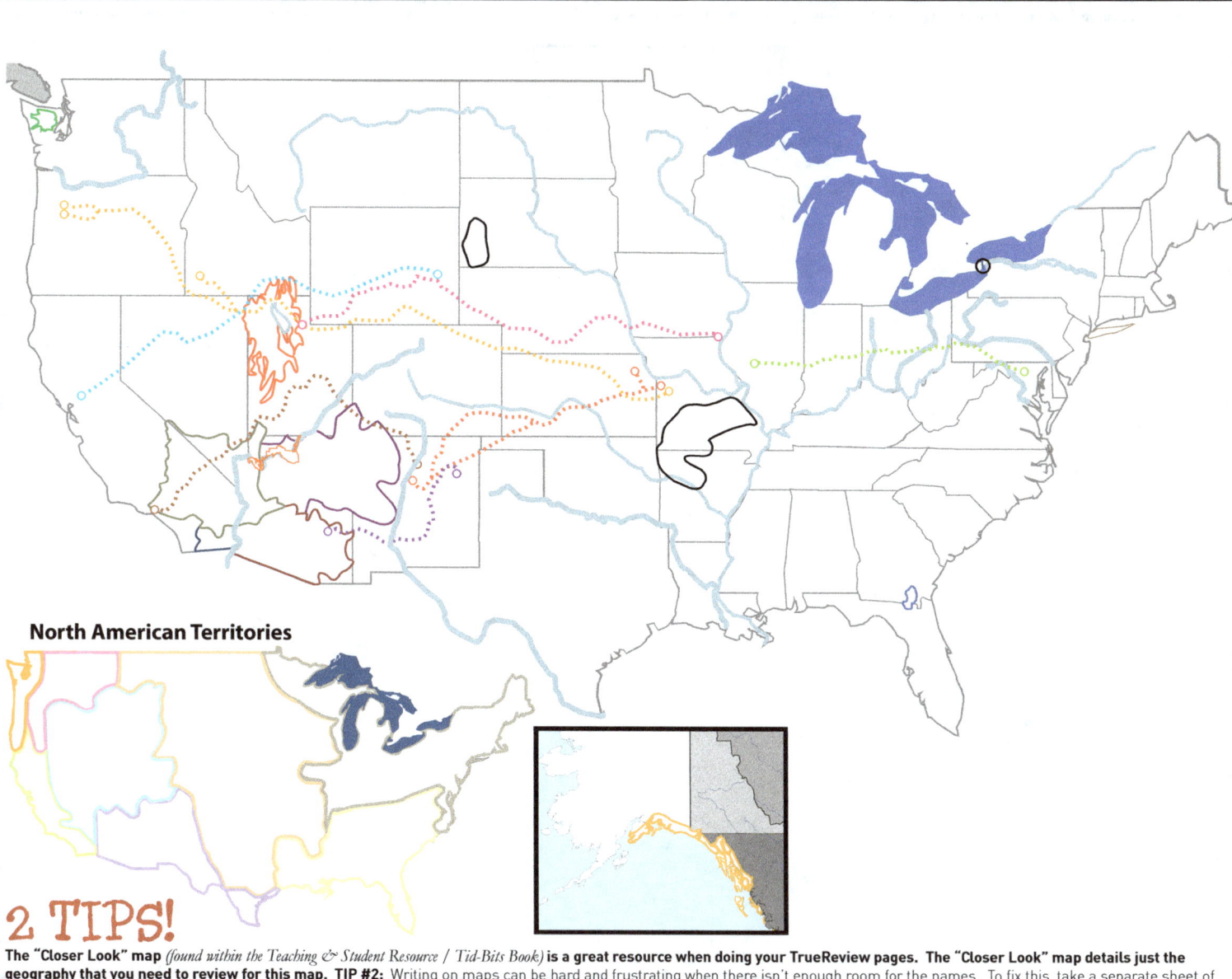

North American Territories

2 TIPS!

The "Closer Look" map *(found within the Teaching & Student Resource / Tid-Bits Book)* **is a great resource when doing your TrueReview pages. The "Closer Look" map details just the geography that you need to review for this map. TIP #2:** Writing on maps can be hard and frustrating when there isn't enough room for the names. To fix this, take a separate sheet of paper and list the geographical names on it, giving each a number. Then, take those numbers and place them in the corresponding geographical area on this map. You can also write the geographic names in a clean space on this page and draw a clean line to the geography that the name belongs to.

Shade & Label all geography from Lessons 17, 18, 19, 20, 21, 22, & 23:

St. Lawrence River
Ohio River
Mississippi River
Missouri River
Arkansas River

Colorado River
Red River
Rio Grande River
Columbia River
Great Salt Lake

Cumberland Road
Santa Fe Trail
Mormon Trail
Gila Trail
Old Spanish Trail
California Trail
Oregon Trail

Erie Canal
Pennsylvania Canal
Chesapeake & Ohio Canal
Ohio & Erie Canal
Miami & Erie Canal

Eastern Woodlands
Plains
Plateau
Northwest Coast
California
Great Basin
Southwest

Mojave Desert
Sonoran Desert
Colorado Desert
Painted Desert
Great Salt Lake Desert

Grand Canyon
Black Hills
Ozark Highlands
Okefenokee Swamp
Olympic Rainforests
Niagara Falls

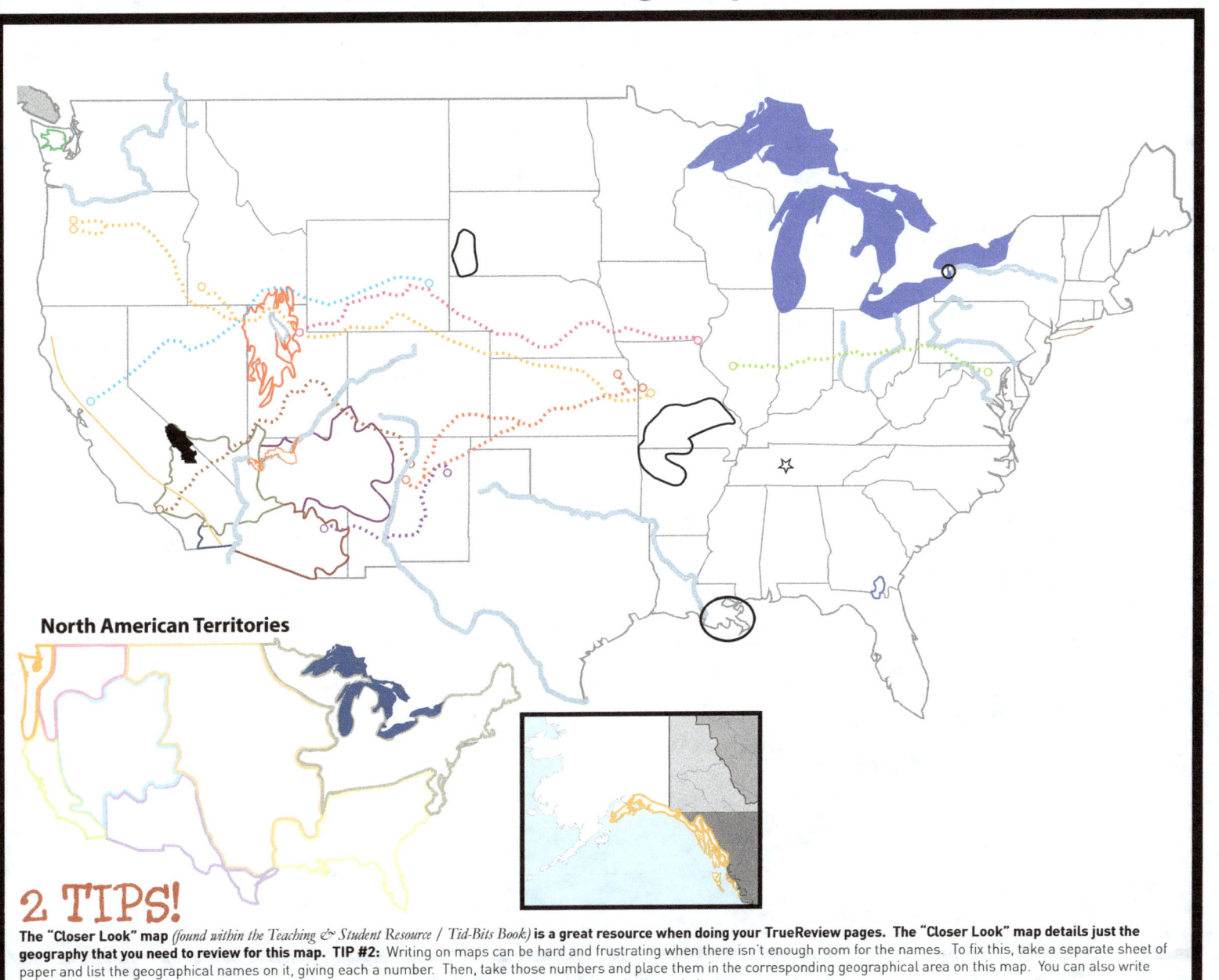

TRUE REVIEW! Memorization Through Repetition — Week 24 REVIEW

Do 2 Of This Map Per Lesson, This Map Is On The Backside Of This Page.

Shade & Label all geography from Lessons 18, 19, 20, 21, 22, 23, & 24:

Colorado River
Red River
Rio Grande River
Columbia River
Great Salt Lake

Cumberland Road
Santa Fe Trail
Mormon Trail
Gila Trail
Old Spanish Trail
California Trail
Oregon Trail

Erie Canal
Pennsylvania Canal
Chesapeake & Ohio Canal
Ohio & Erie Canal
Miami & Erie Canal

Eastern Woodlands
Plains
Plateau
Northwest Coast
California
Great Basin
Southwest

Mojave Desert
Sonoran Desert
Colorado Desert
Painted Desert
Great Salt Lake Desert

Grand Canyon
Black Hills
Ozark Highlands
Okefenokee Swamp
Olympic Rainforests
Niagara Falls

Mississippi River Delta
Mammoth Cave
San Andreas Fault
Gulf of Mexico
Death Valley

North American Territories

2 TIPS!

The "Closer Look" map *(found within the Teaching & Student Resource / Tid-Bits Book)* **is a great resource when doing your TrueReview pages. The "Closer Look" map details just the geography that you need to review for this map. TIP #2:** Writing on maps can be hard and frustrating when there isn't enough room for the names. To fix this, take a separate sheet of paper and list the geographical names on it, giving each a number. Then, take those numbers and place them in the corresponding geographical area on this map. You can also write the geographic names in a clean space on this page and draw a clean line to the geography that the name belongs to.

TRUE REVIEW! Memorization Through Repetition

Do 2 Of This Map Per Lesson, This Map Is On The Backside Of This Page.

Week 24 REVIEW

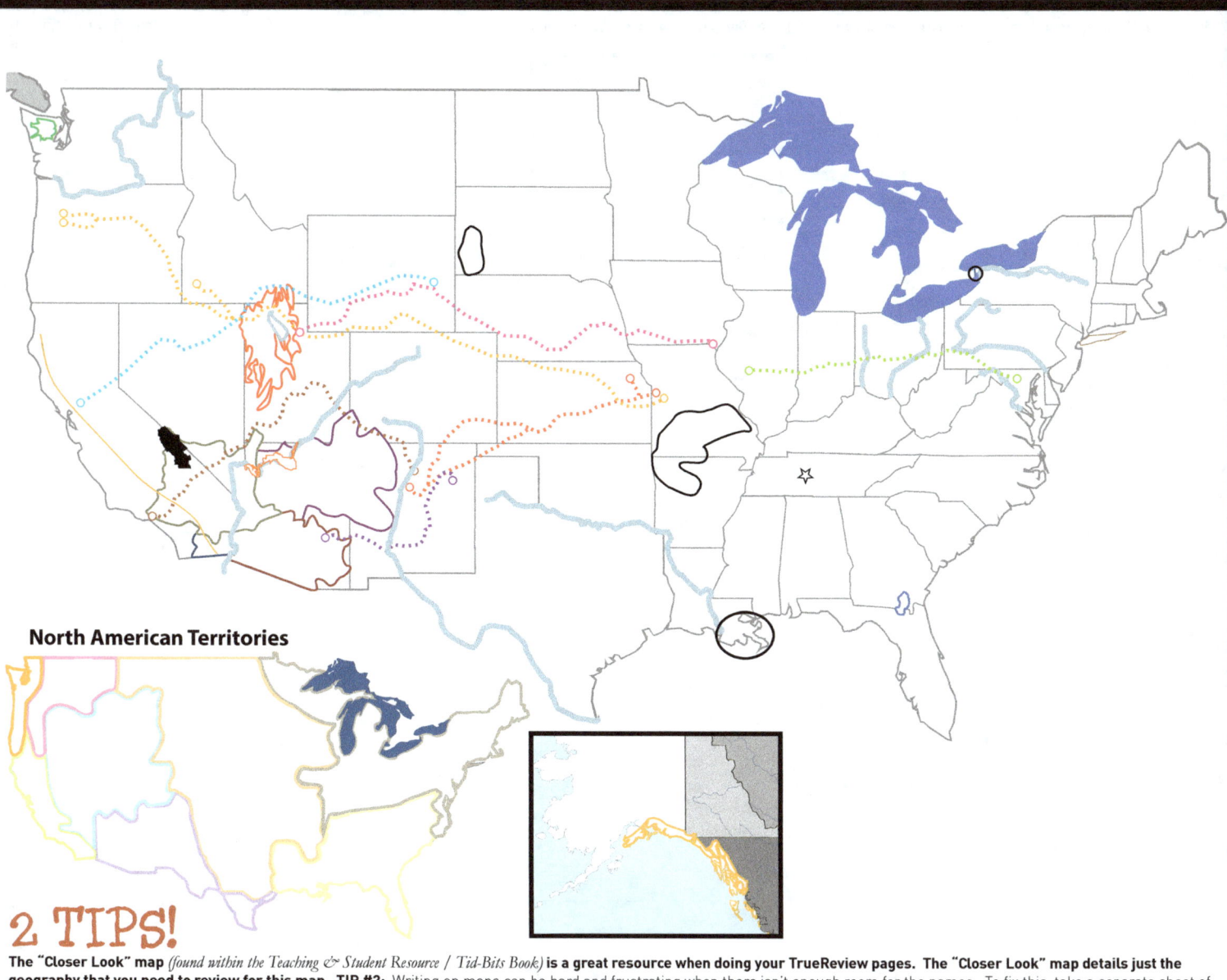

North American Territories

2 TIPS!

The "Closer Look" map *(found within the Teaching & Student Resource / Tid-Bits Book)* **is a great resource when doing your TrueReview pages. The "Closer Look" map details just the geography that you need to review for this map. TIP #2:** Writing on maps can be hard and frustrating when there isn't enough room for the names. To fix this, take a separate sheet of paper and list the geographical names on it, giving each a number. Then, take those numbers and place them in the corresponding geographical area on this map. You can also write the geographic names in a clean space on this page and draw a clean line to the geography that the name belongs to.

Shade & Label all geography from Lessons 18, 19, 20, 21, 22, 23, & 24:

Colorado River
Red River
Rio Grande River
Columbia River
Great Salt Lake

Cumberland Road
Santa Fe Trail
Mormon Trail
Gila Trail
Old Spanish Trail
California Trail
Oregon Trail

Erie Canal
Pennsylvania Canal
Chesapeake & Ohio Canal
Ohio & Erie Canal
Miami & Erie Canal

Eastern Woodlands
Plains
Plateau
Northwest Coast
California
Great Basin
Southwest

Mojave Desert
Sonoran Desert
Colorado Desert
Painted Desert
Great Salt Lake Desert

Grand Canyon
Black Hills
Ozark Highlands
Okefenokee Swamp
Olympic Rainforests
Niagara Falls

Mississippi River Delta
Mammoth Cave
San Andreas Fault
Gulf of Mexico
Death Valley

TRUE REVIEW! Memorization Through Repetition

Do 2 Of This Map Per Lesson, This Map Is On The Backside Of This Page.

Week 25 REVIEW

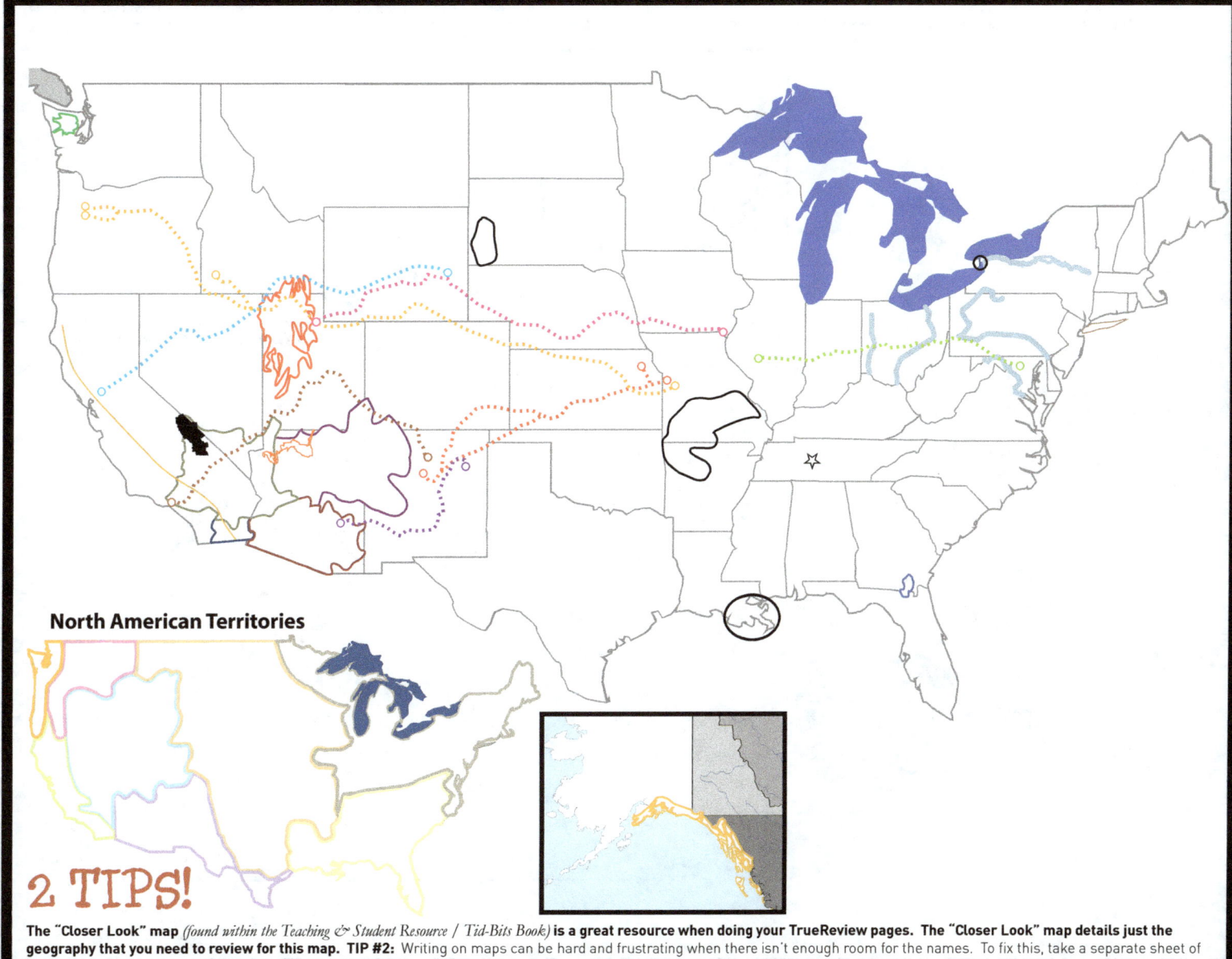

Shade & Label all geography from Lessons 19, 20, 21, 22, 23, & 24:

Cumberland Road
Santa Fe Trail
Mormon Trail
Gila Trail
Old Spanish Trail
California Trail
Oregon Trail

Erie Canal
Pennsylvania Canal
Chesapeake & Ohio Canal
Ohio & Erie Canal
Miami & Erie Canal

Eastern Woodlands
Plains
Plateau
Northwest Coast
California
Great Basin
Southwest

Mojave Desert
Sonoran Desert
Colorado Desert
Painted Desert
Great Salt Lake Desert

Grand Canyon
Black Hills
Ozark Highlands
Okefenokee Swamp
Olympic Rainforests
Niagara Falls

Mississippi River Delta
Mammoth Cave
San Andreas Fault
Gulf of Mexico
Death Valley

North American Territories

2 TIPS!

The "Closer Look" map *(found within the Teaching & Student Resource / Tid-Bits Book)* is a great resource when doing your TrueReview pages. The "Closer Look" map details just the geography that you need to review for this map. **TIP #2:** Writing on maps can be hard and frustrating when there isn't enough room for the names. To fix this, take a separate sheet of paper and list the geographical names on it, giving each a number. Then, take those numbers and place them in the corresponding geographical area on this map. You can also write the geographic names in a clean space on this page and draw a clean line to the geography that the name belongs to.

TRUE REVIEW! Memorization Through Repetition

Do 2 Of This Map Per Lesson, This Map Is On The Backside Of This Page.

Week 25 REVIEW

Shade & Label all geography from Lessons 19, 20, 21, 22, 23, & 24:

Cumberland Road
Santa Fe Trail
Mormon Trail
Gila Trail
Old Spanish Trail
California Trail
Oregon Trail

Erie Canal
Pennsylvania Canal
Chesapeake & Ohio Canal
Ohio & Erie Canal
Miami & Erie Canal

Eastern Woodlands
Plains
Plateau
Northwest Coast
California
Great Basin
Southwest

Mojave Desert
Sonoran Desert
Colorado Desert
Painted Desert
Great Salt Lake Desert

Grand Canyon
Black Hills
Ozark Highlands
Okefenokee Swamp
Olympic Rainforests
Niagara Falls

Mississippi River Delta
Mammoth Cave
San Andreas Fault
Gulf of Mexico
Death Valley

North American Territories

2 TIPS!

The "Closer Look" map *(found within the Teaching & Student Resource / Tid-Bits Book)* **is a great resource when doing your TrueReview pages. The "Closer Look" map details just the geography that you need to review for this map. TIP #2:** Writing on maps can be hard and frustrating when there isn't enough room for the names. To fix this, take a separate sheet of paper and list the geographical names on it, giving each a number. Then, take those numbers and place them in the corresponding geographical area on this map. You can also write the geographic names in a clean space on this page and draw a clean line to the geography that the name belongs to.

TRUE REVIEW! Memorization Through Repetition

Do 2 Of This Map Per Lesson, This Map Is On The Backside Of This Page.

Week 26 REVIEW

Shade & Label all geography from Lessons 20, 21, 22, 23, & 24:

Erie Canal
Pennsylvania Canal
Chesapeake & Ohio Canal
Ohio & Erie Canal
Miami & Erie Canal

Eastern Woodlands
Plains
Plateau
Northwest Coast
California
Great Basin
Southwest

Mojave Desert
Sonoran Desert
Colorado Desert
Painted Desert
Great Salt Lake Desert

Grand Canyon
Black Hills
Ozark Highlands
Okefenokee Swamp
Olympic Rainforests
Niagara Falls

Mississippi River Delta
Mammoth Cave
San Andreas Fault
Gulf of Mexico
Death Valley

North American Territories

2 TIPS!

The "Closer Look" map *(found within the Teaching & Student Resource / Tid-Bits Book)* **is a great resource when doing your TrueReview pages. The "Closer Look" map details just the geography that you need to review for this map.** **TIP #2:** Writing on maps can be hard and frustrating when there isn't enough room for the names. To fix this, take a separate sheet of paper and list the geographical names on it, giving each a number. Then, take those numbers and place them in the corresponding geographical area on this map. You can also write the geographic names in a clean space on this page and draw a clean line to the geography that the name belongs to.

TRUE REVIEW! Memorization Through Repetition

Do 2 Of This Map Per Lesson, This Map Is On The Backside Of This Page.

Week 26 REVIEW

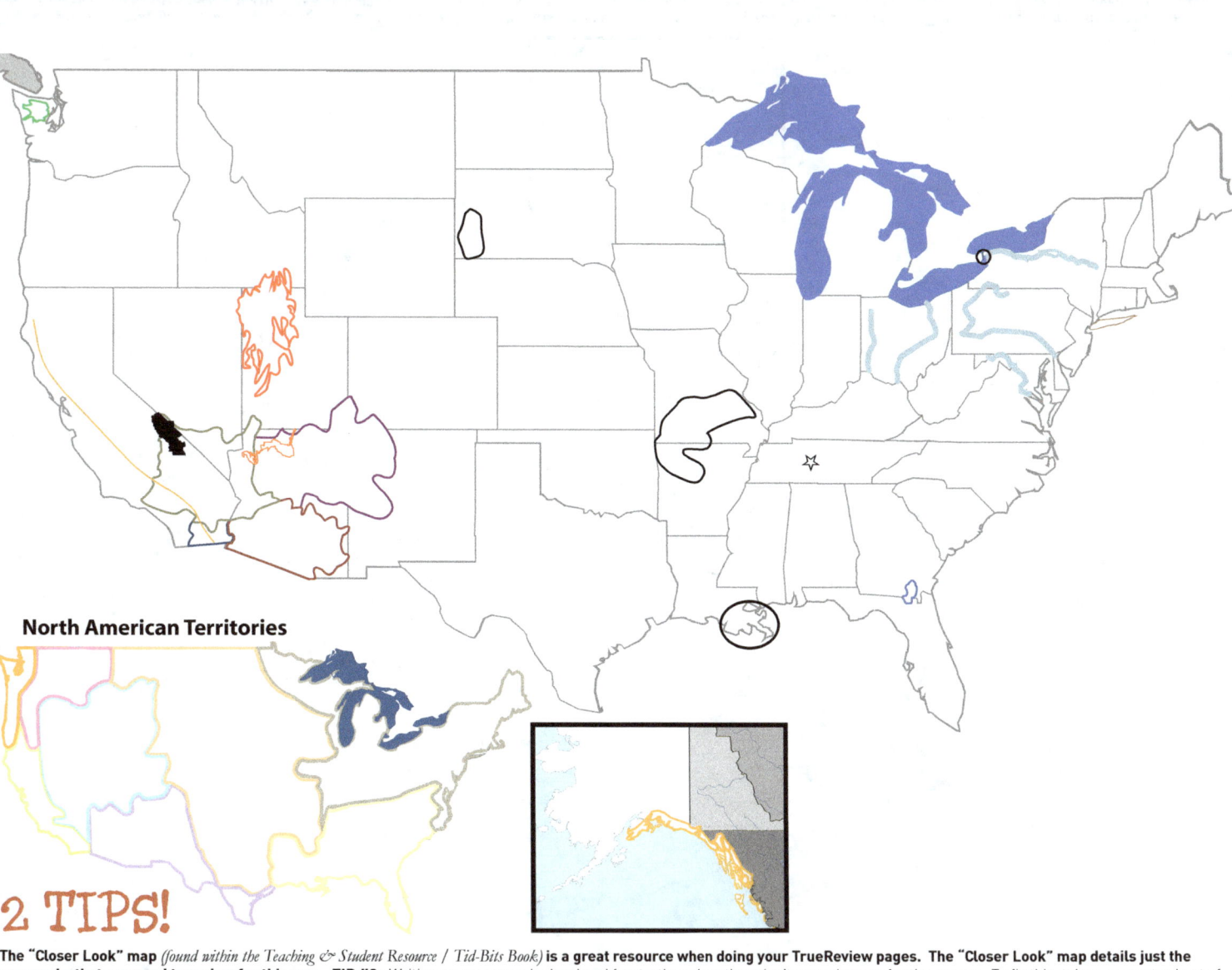

North American Territories

2 TIPS!

Shade & Label all geography from Lessons 20, 21, 22, 23, & 24:

Erie Canal
Pennsylvania Canal
Chesapeake & Ohio Canal
Ohio & Erie Canal
Miami & Erie Canal

Eastern Woodlands
Plains
Plateau
Northwest Coast
California
Great Basin
Southwest

Mojave Desert
Sonoran Desert
Colorado Desert
Painted Desert
Great Salt Lake Desert

Grand Canyon
Black Hills
Ozark Highlands
Okefenokee Swamp
Olympic Rainforests
Niagara Falls

Mississippi River Delta
Mammoth Cave
San Andreas Fault
Gulf of Mexico
Death Valley

The **"Closer Look" map** *(found within the Teaching & Student Resource / Tid-Bits Book)* **is a great resource when doing your TrueReview pages. The "Closer Look" map details just the geography that you need to review for this map. TIP #2:** Writing on maps can be hard and frustrating when there isn't enough room for the names. To fix this, take a separate sheet of paper and list the geographical names on it, giving each a number. Then, take those numbers and place them in the corresponding geographical area on this map. You can also write the geographic names in a clean space on this page and draw a clean line to the geography that the name belongs to.

TRUE REVIEW! Memorization Through Repetition

Do 2 Of This Map Per Lesson, This Map Is On The Backside Of This Page.

Week 27 REVIEW

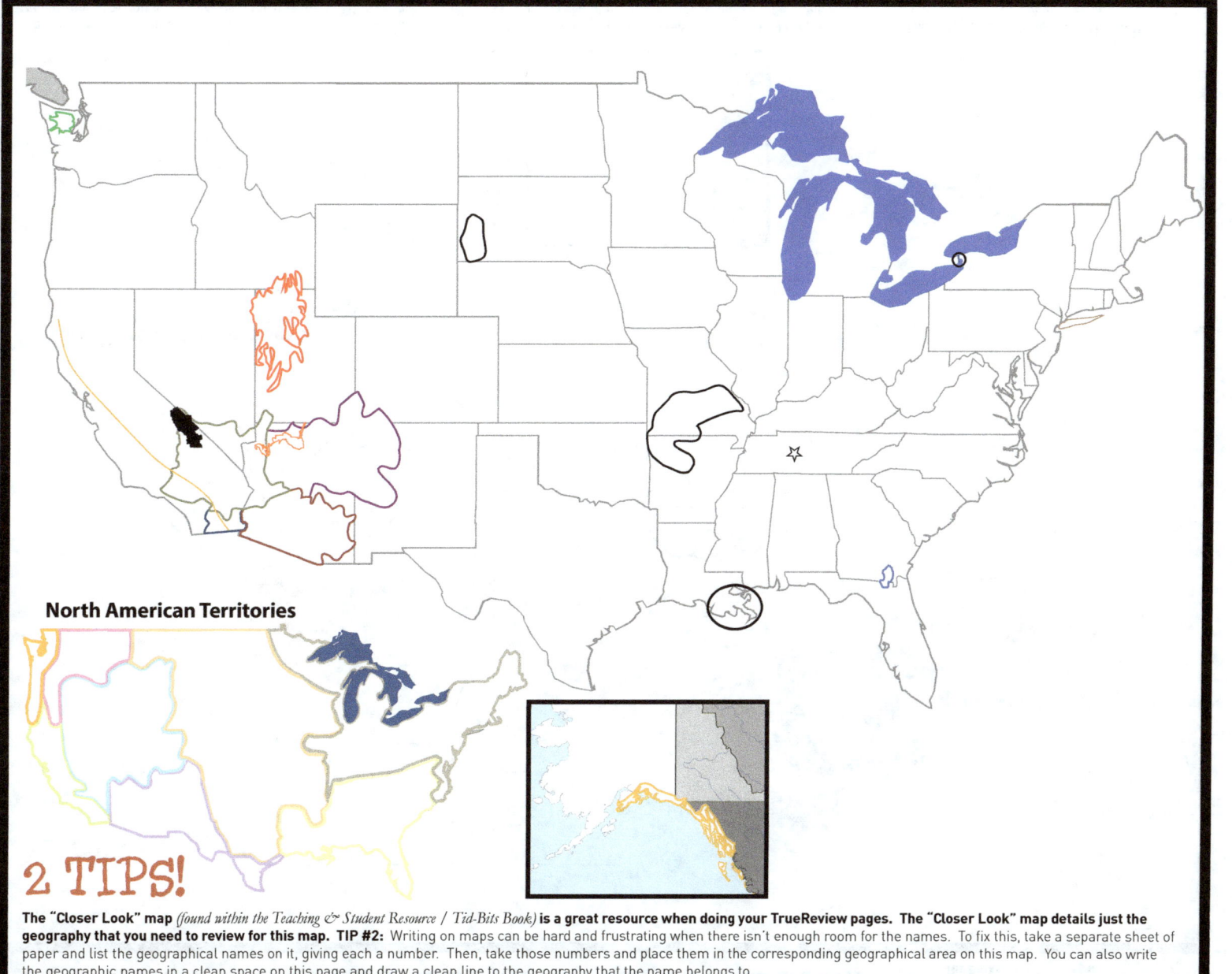

Shade & Label all geography from Lessons 21, 22, 23, & 24:

Eastern Woodlands
Plains
Plateau
Northwest Coast
California
Great Basin
Southwest

Mojave Desert
Sonoran Desert
Colorado Desert
Painted Desert
Great Salt Lake Desert

Grand Canyon
Black Hills
Ozark Highlands
Okefenokee Swamp
Olympic Rainforests
Niagara Falls

Mississippi River Delta
Mammoth Cave
San Andreas Fault
Gulf of Mexico
Death Valley

North American Territories

2 TIPS!

The "Closer Look" map *(found within the Teaching & Student Resource / Tid-Bits Book)* **is a great resource when doing your TrueReview pages. The "Closer Look" map details just the geography that you need to review for this map. TIP #2:** Writing on maps can be hard and frustrating when there isn't enough room for the names. To fix this, take a separate sheet of paper and list the geographical names on it, giving each a number. Then, take those numbers and place them in the corresponding geographical area on this map. You can also write the geographic names in a clean space on this page and draw a clean line to the geography that the name belongs to.

TRUE REVIEW! Memorization Through Repetition

Do 2 Of This Map Per Lesson, This Map Is On The Backside Of This Page.

Week 27 REVIEW

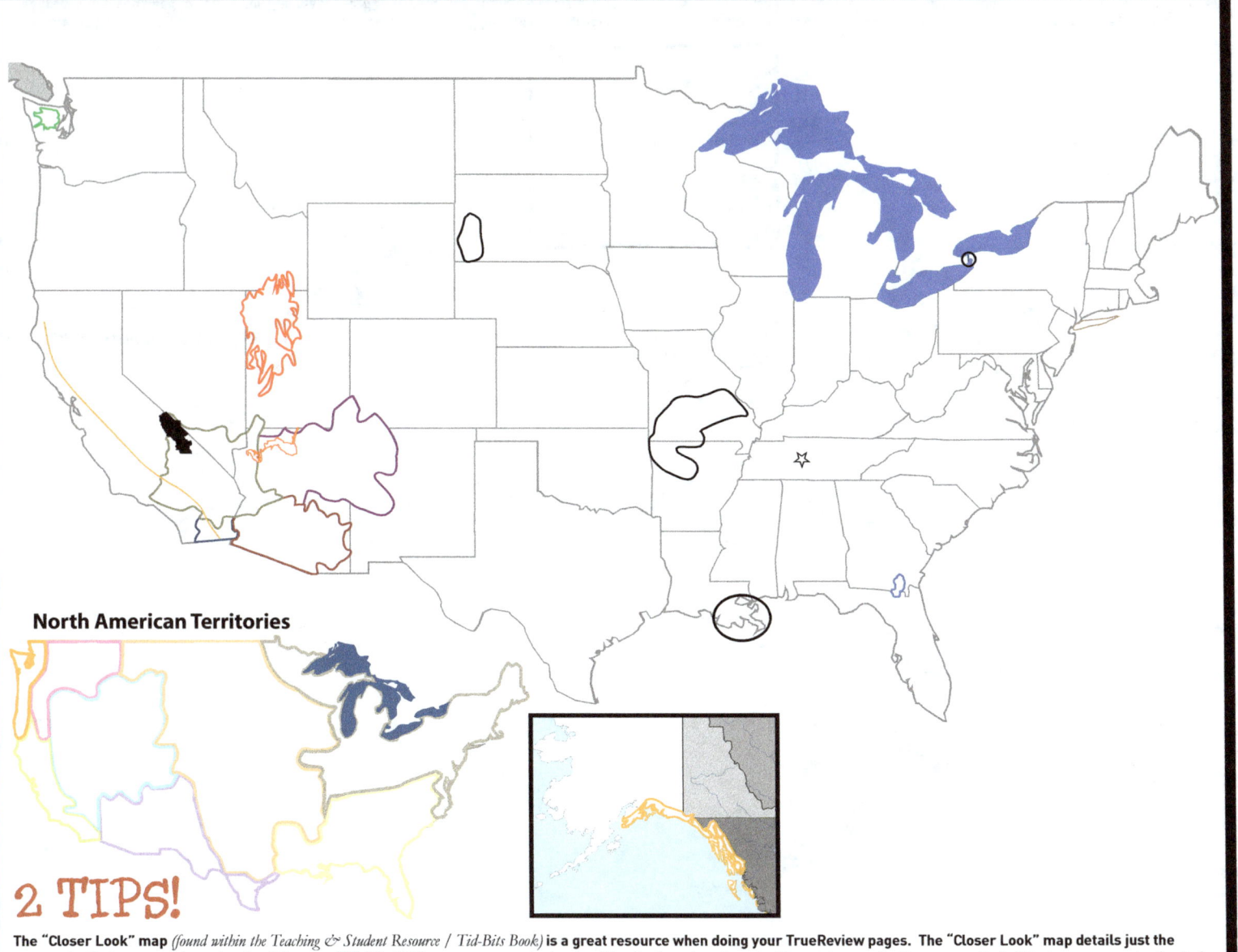

North American Territories

2 TIPS!

Shade & Label all geography from Lessons 21, 22, 23, & 24:

Eastern Woodlands
Plains
Plateau
Northwest Coast
California
Great Basin
Southwest

Mojave Desert
Sonoran Desert
Colorado Desert
Painted Desert
Great Salt Lake Desert

Grand Canyon
Black Hills
Ozark Highlands
Okefenokee Swamp
Olympic Rainforests
Niagara Falls

Mississippi River Delta
Mammoth Cave
San Andreas Fault
Gulf of Mexico
Death Valley

The "Closer Look" map *(found within the Teaching & Student Resource / Tid-Bits Book)* **is a great resource when doing your TrueReview pages. The "Closer Look" map details just the geography that you need to review for this map. TIP #2:** Writing on maps can be hard and frustrating when there isn't enough room for the names. To fix this, take a separate sheet of paper and list the geographical names on it, giving each a number. Then, take those numbers and place them in the corresponding geographical area on this map. You can also write the geographic names in a clean space on this page and draw a clean line to the geography that the name belongs to.

TRUE REVIEW! Memorization Through Repetition

Do 2 Of This Map Per Lesson, This Map Is On The Backside Of This Page.

Week 28 REVIEW

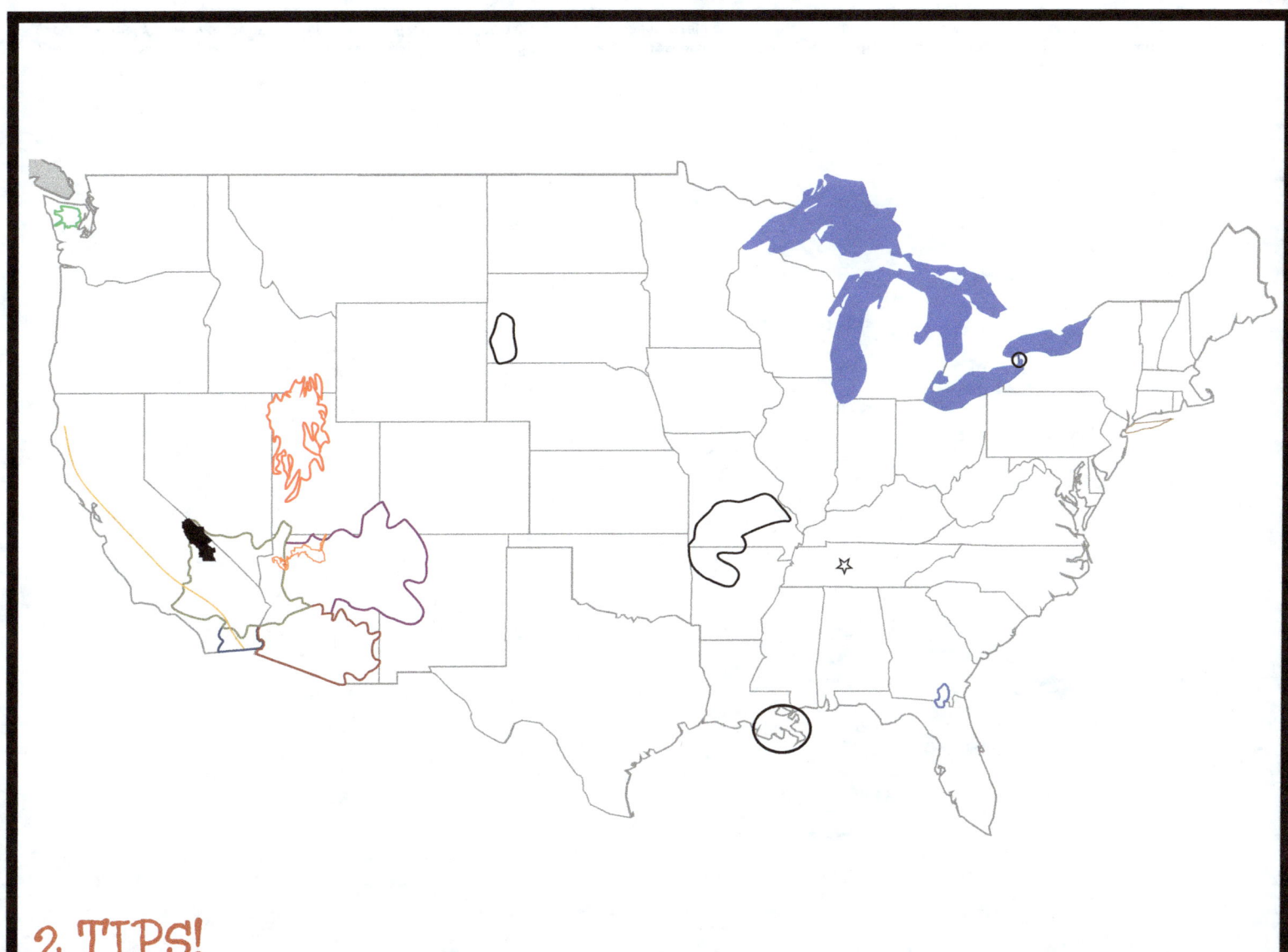

Shade & Label all geography from Lessons 22, 23, & 24:

Mojave Desert
Sonoran Desert
Colorado Desert
Painted Desert
Great Salt Lake Desert

Grand Canyon
Black Hills
Ozark Highlands
Okefenokee Swamp
Olympic Rainforests
Niagara Falls

Mississippi River Delta
Mammoth Cave
San Andreas Fault
Gulf of Mexico
Death Valley

2 TIPS!

The "Closer Look" map *(found within the Teaching & Student Resource / Tid-Bits Book)* **is a great resource when doing your TrueReview pages. The "Closer Look" map details just the geography that you need to review for this map. TIP #2:** Writing on maps can be hard and frustrating when there isn't enough room for the names. To fix this, take a separate sheet of paper and list the geographical names on it, giving each a number. Then, take those numbers and place them in the corresponding geographical area on this map. You can also write the geographic names in a clean space on this page and draw a clean line to the geography that the name belongs to.

105

TRUE REVIEW! Memorization Through Repetition

Do 2 Of This Map Per Lesson, This Map Is On The Backside Of This Page.

Week 28 REVIEW

Shade & Label all geography from Lessons 22, 23, & 24:

Mojave Desert
Sonoran Desert
Colorado Desert
Painted Desert
Great Salt Lake Desert

Grand Canyon
Black Hills
Ozark Highlands
Okefenokee Swamp
Olympic Rainforests
Niagara Falls

Mississippi River Delta
Mammoth Cave
San Andreas Fault
Gulf of Mexico
Death Valley

2 TIPS!

The "Closer Look" map *(found within the Teaching & Student Resource / Tid-Bits Book)* **is a great resource when doing your TrueReview pages. The "Closer Look" map details just the geography that you need to review for this map. TIP #2:** Writing on maps can be hard and frustrating when there isn't enough room for the names. To fix this, take a separate sheet of paper and list the geographical names on it, giving each a number. Then, take those numbers and place them in the corresponding geographical area on this map. You can also write the geographic names in a clean space on this page and draw a clean line to the geography that the name belongs to.

TRUE REVIEW! Memorization Through Repetition

Do 2 Of This Map Per Lesson, This Map Is On The Backside Of This Page.

Week 29 REVIEW

Shade & Label all geography from Lessons 23, & 24:

Grand Canyon
Black Hills
Ozark Highlands
Okefenokee Swamp
Olympic Rainforests
Niagara Falls

Mississippi River Delta
Mammoth Cave
San Andreas Fault
Gulf of Mexico
Death Valley

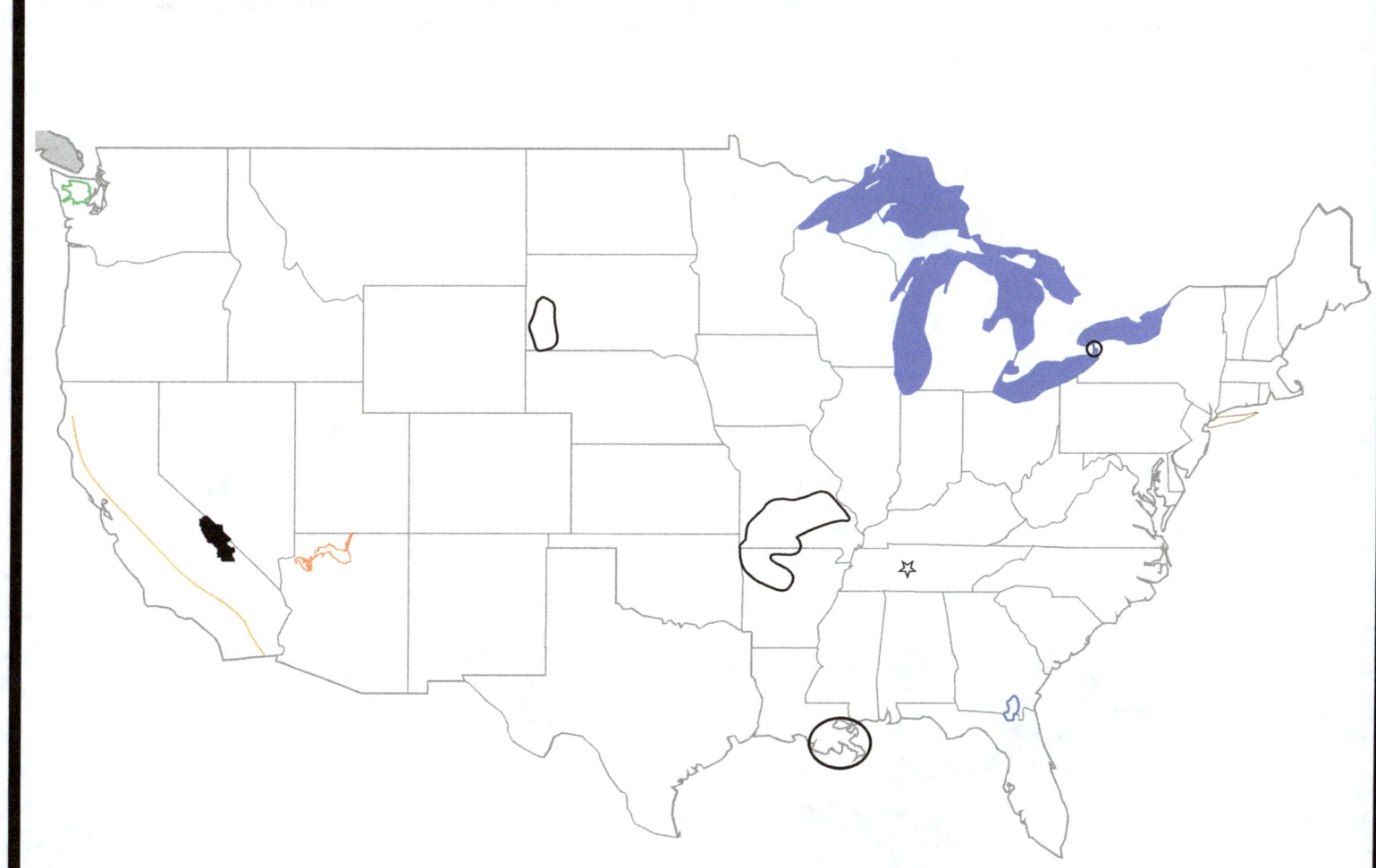

2 TIPS!

The "Closer Look" map *(found within the Teaching & Student Resource / Tid-Bits Book)* **is a great resource when doing your TrueReview pages. The "Closer Look" map details just the geography that you need to review for this map. TIP #2:** Writing on maps can be hard and frustrating when there isn't enough room for the names. To fix this, take a separate sheet of paper and list the geographical names on it, giving each a number. Then, take those numbers and place them in the corresponding geographical area on this map. You can also write the geographic names in a clean space on this page and draw a clean line to the geography that the name belongs to.

TRUE REVIEW! Memorization Through Repetition

Do 2 Of This Map Per Lesson, This Map Is On The Backside Of This Page.

Week 29 REVIEW

Shade & Label all geography from Lessons 23, & 24:

Grand Canyon
Black Hills
Ozark Highlands
Okefenokee Swamp
Olympic Rainforests
Niagara Falls

Mississippi River Delta
Mammoth Cave
San Andreas Fault
Gulf of Mexico
Death Valley

2 TIPS!

The "Closer Look" map *(found within the Teaching & Student Resource / Tid-Bits Book)* **is a great resource when doing your TrueReview pages. The "Closer Look" map details just the geography that you need to review for this map. TIP #2:** Writing on maps can be hard and frustrating when there isn't enough room for the names. To fix this, take a separate sheet of paper and list the geographical names on it, giving each a number. Then, take those numbers and place them in the corresponding geographical area on this map. You can also write the geographic names in a clean space on this page and draw a clean line to the geography that the name belongs to.

TRUE REVIEW! Memorization Through Repetition

Do 2 Of This Map Per Lesson, This Map Is On The Backside Of This Page.

Week 30 REVIEW

Shade & Label all geography from Lesson 24:

Mississippi River Delta
Mammoth Cave
San Andreas Fault
Gulf of Mexico
Death Valley

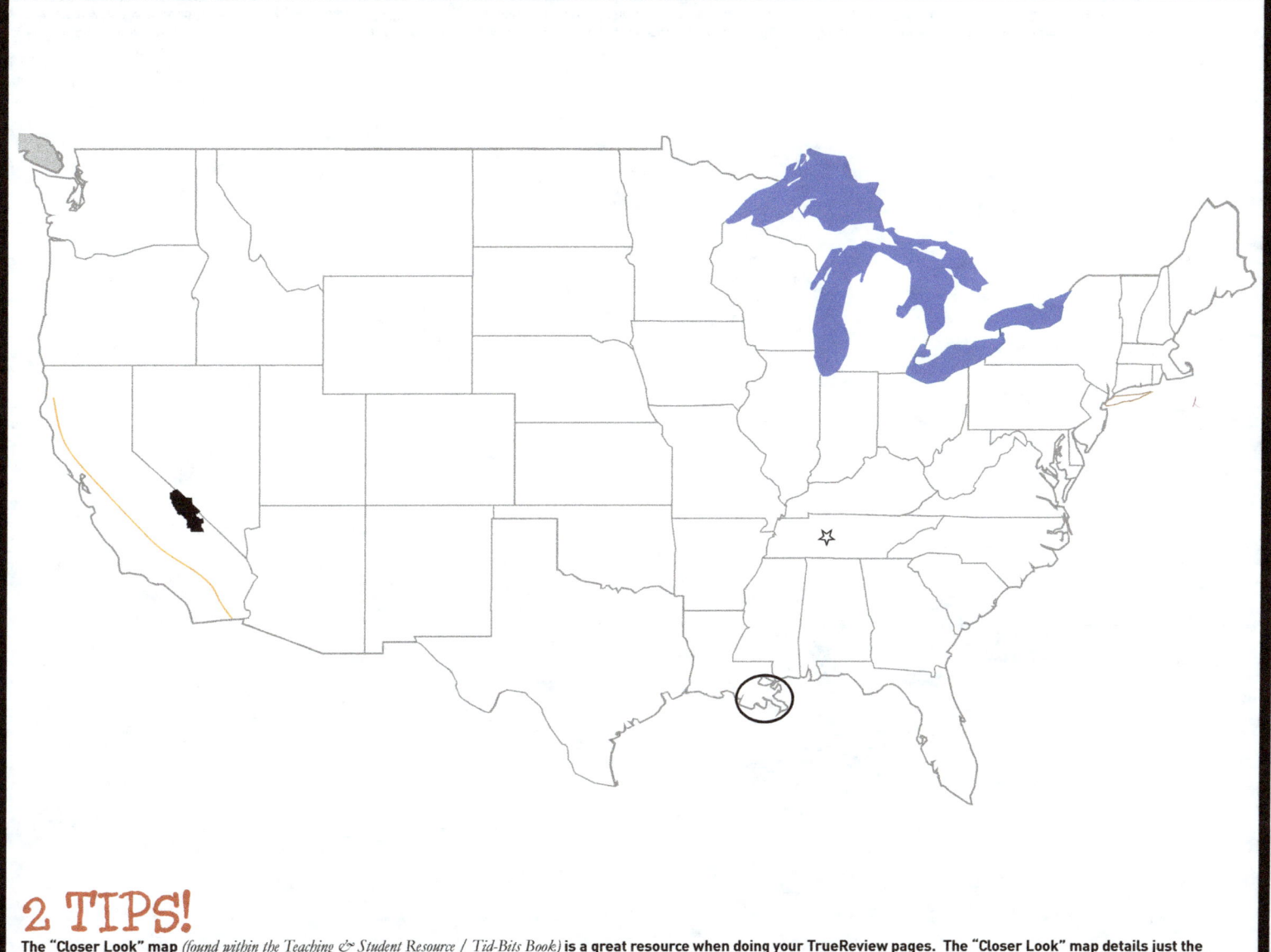

2 TIPS!

The "Closer Look" map *(found within the Teaching & Student Resource / Tid-Bits Book)* **is a great resource when doing your TrueReview pages. The "Closer Look" map details just the geography that you need to review for this map. TIP #2:** Writing on maps can be hard and frustrating when there isn't enough room for the names. To fix this, take a separate sheet of paper and list the geographical names on it, giving each a number. Then, take those numbers and place them in the corresponding geographical area on this map. You can also write the geographic names in a clean space on this page and draw a clean line to the geography that the name belongs to.

TRUE REVIEW! Memorization Through Repetition

Do 2 Of This Map Per Lesson, This Map Is On The Backside Of This Page.

Week 30 REVIEW

Shade & Label all geography from Lesson 24:

Mississippi River Delta
Mammoth Cave
San Andreas Fault
Gulf of Mexico
Death Valley

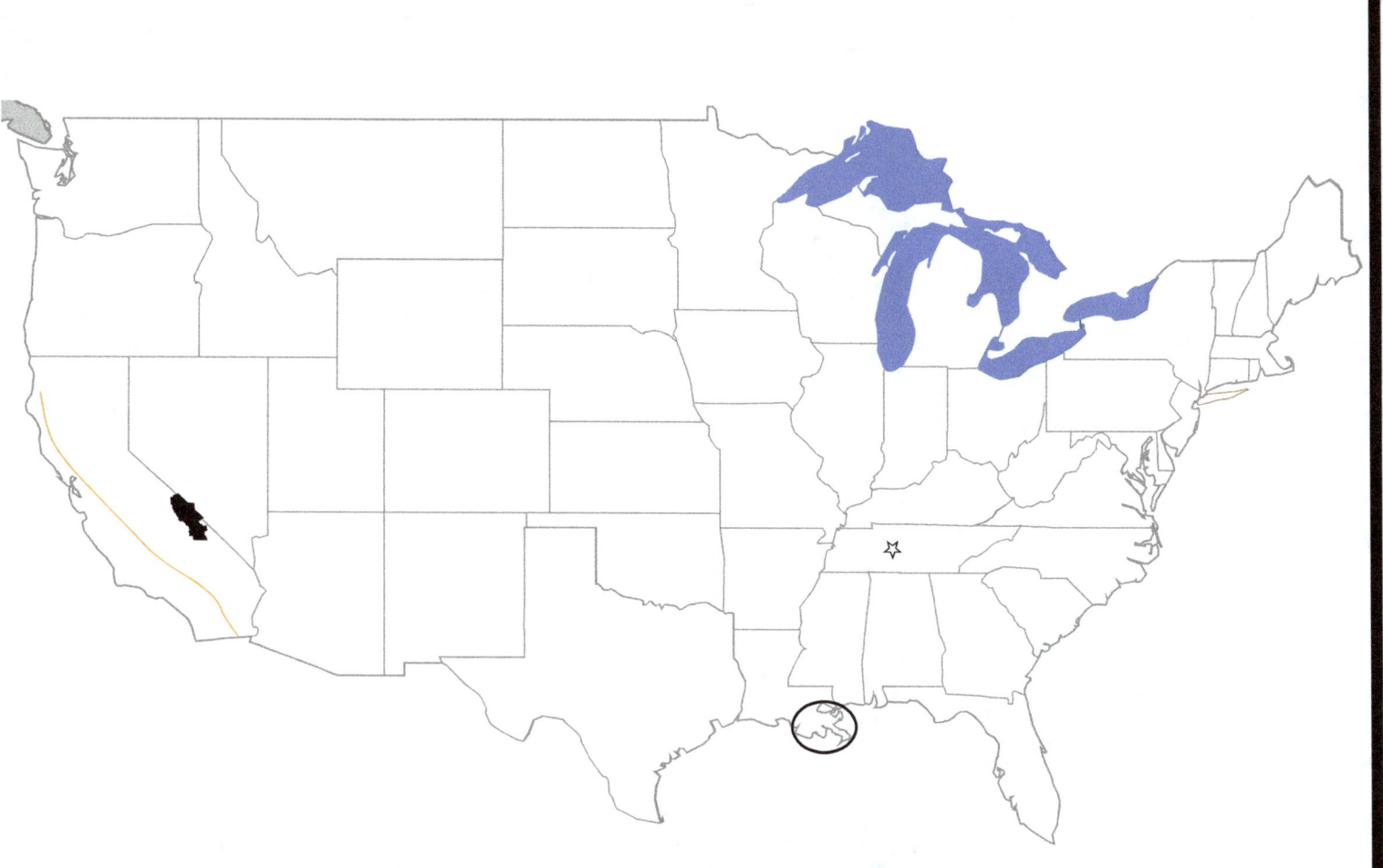

2 TIPS!

The "Closer Look" map *(found within the Teaching & Student Resource / Tid-Bits Book)* **is a great resource when doing your TrueReview pages. The "Closer Look" map details just the geography that you need to review for this map. TIP #2:** Writing on maps can be hard and frustrating when there isn't enough room for the names. To fix this, take a separate sheet of paper and list the geographical names on it, giving each a number. Then, take those numbers and place them in the corresponding geographical area on this map. You can also write the geographic names in a clean space on this page and draw a clean line to the geography that the name belongs to.

Teaching Aides
Pull-out Maps for posting and copying

Summary Map for Lessons 1-10
Blank Summary Map for Lessons 1-10

Summary Map for Lessons 11-17
Blank Summary Map for Lessons 11-17

Summary Map for Lessons 18-24
Blank Summary Map for Lessons 18-24

View of the United States Capitol Building in Washington, DC at dusk.

Summary Map for Lessons 1-10

Lesson 1
Augusta, Maine (ME)
Concord, New Hampshire (NH)
Boston, Massachusettes (MA)
Providence, Rhode Island (RI)
Hartford, Conecticut (CT)

Lesson 2
Montpelier, Vermont (VT)
Albany, New York (NY)
Trenton, New Jersey (NJ)
Harrisburg, Pennsylvania (PA)
Dover, Delaware (DE)

Lesson 3
Annapolis, Maryland (MD)
Richmond, Virginia (VA)
Charleston, West Virginia (WV)
Raleigh, North Carolina (NC)
Columbia, South Carolina (SC)
Washington, D.C.

Lesson 4
Atlanta, Georgia (GA)
Tallahassee, Florida, (FL)
Montgomery, Alabama (AL)
Jackson, Mississippi (MS)
Baton Rouge, Louisiana (LA)

Lesson 5
Lansing, Michigan (MI)
Columbus, Ohio (OH)
Indianapolis, Indiana (IN)
Frankfort, Kentucky (KY)
Nashville, Tennessee (TN)

Lesson 6
Madison, Wisconsin (WI)
Springfield, Illinois (IL)
Des Moines, Iowa (IA)
Jefferson City, Missouri (MO)
Little Rock, Arkansas (AR)

Lesson 7
St. Paul, Minnesota (MN)
Bismarck, North Dakota (ND)
Pierre, South Dakota (SD)
Cheyenne, Wyoming (WY)
Lincoln, Nebraska (NE)

Lesson 8
Topeka, Kansas (KS)
Oklahoma City, Okoahoma (OK)
Austin, Texas (TX)
Denver, Colorado (CO)
Santa Fe, New Mexico (NM)

Lesson 9
Salt Lake City, Utah (UT)
Phoenix, Arizona (AZ)
Carson City, Nevada (NV)
Sacramento, California (CA)
Honolulu, Hawaii (HI)

Lesson 10
Helena, Montana (MT)
Boise, Idaho (ID)
Olympia, Washington (WA)
Salem, Oregon (OR)
Juneau, Alaska (AK)

113

Blank Master Summary Map - Lessons 1-10

Summary Map Lessons 11-17

Lesson 11
Northern Appalachians

White Mountains
Green Mountains
Adirondack Mountains
Allegheny Mountains

Lesson 12
Southern Appalachians

The Great Valley
Blue Ridge Mountains
Great Smoky Mountains
Cumberland Mountains
Mt. Mitchell

Lesson 13
Western Mountains

Rocky Mountains
Pikes Peak
Mt. Elbert
Sierra Nevada
Mt. Whitney

Lesson 14
Northwest Mountains

Cascade Mountains
Mt. Rainier
Mt. St. Helens
Denali

Lesson 15
Great Lakes

Lake Huron
Lake Ontario
Lake Michigan
Lake Erie
Lake Superior

Lesson 16
Bays & Sounds

Chesapeake Bay
Hudson Bay (Canada)
San Francisco Bay
Puget Sound
Pamlico Sound

Lesson 17
Eastern Rivers

St. Lawrence River
Ohio River
Mississippi River
Missouri River
Arkansas River

115

Blank Summary Map Lessons 11-17

Lesson 11
Northern Appalachians

White Mountains
Green Mountains
Adirondack Mountains
Allegheny Mountains

Lesson 12
Southern Appalachians

The Great Valley
Blue Ridge Mountains
Great Smoky Mountains
Cumberland Mountains
Mt. Mitchell

Lesson 13
Western Mountains

Rocky Mountains
Pikes Peak
Mt. Elbert
Sierra Nevada
Mt. Whitney

Lesson 14
Northwest Mountains

Cascade Mountains
Mt. Rainier
Mt. St. Helens
Denali

Lesson 15
Great Lakes

Lake Huron
Lake Ontario
Lake Michigan
Lake Erie
Lake Superior

Lesson 16
Bays & Sounds

Chesapeake Bay
Hudson Bay (Canada)
San Francisco Bay
Puget Sound
Pamlico Sound

Lesson 17
Eastern Rivers

St. Lawrence River
Ohio River
Mississippi River
Missouri River
Arkansas River

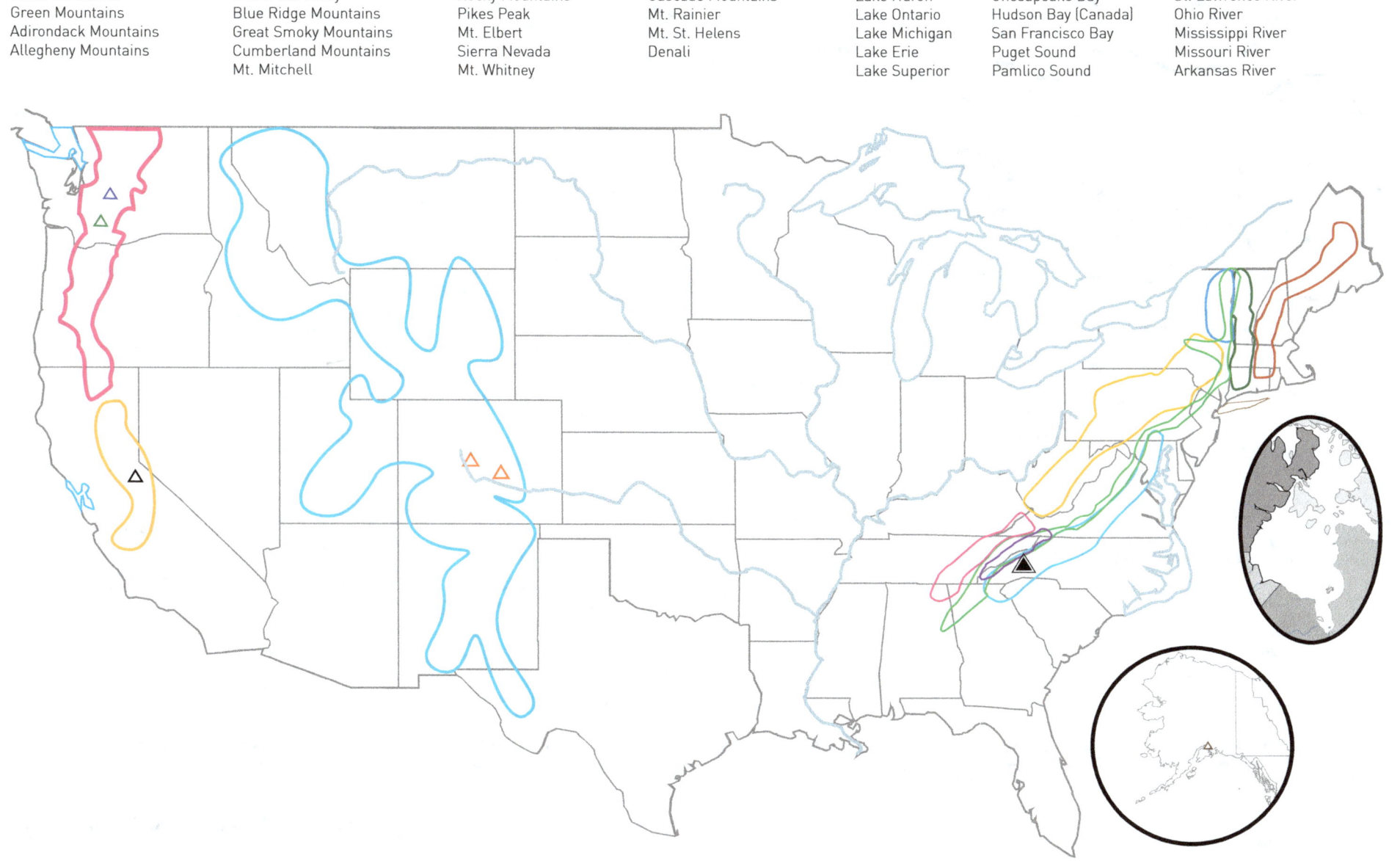

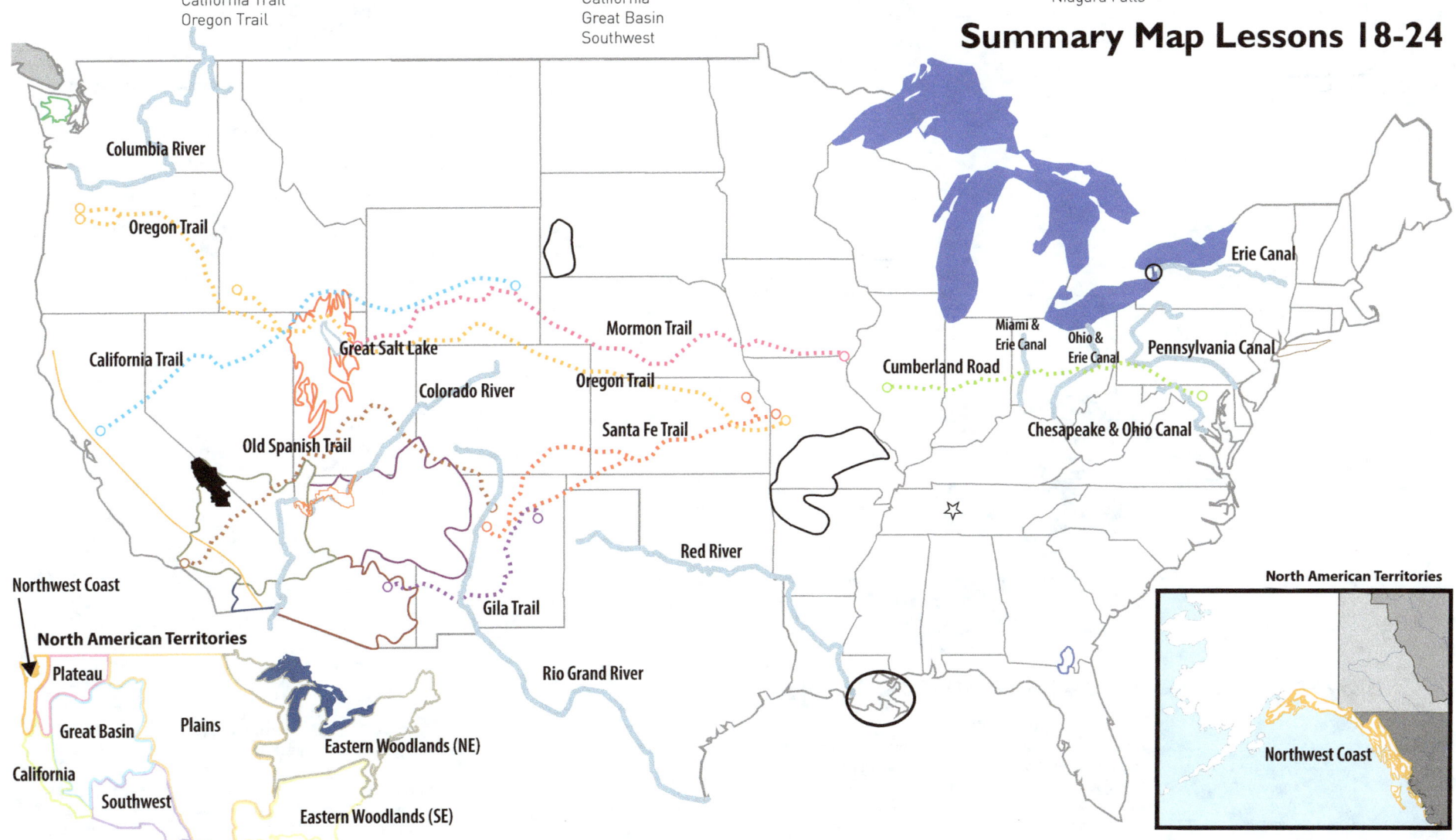

Summary Map Lessons 18-24

Lesson 18 — Western Rivers
- Colorado River
- Red River
- Rio Grande River
- Columbia River
- Great Salt Lake

Lesson 19 — Historic Trails
- Cumberland Road
- Santa Fe Trail
- Mormon Trail
- Gila Trail
- Old Spanish Trail
- California Trail
- Oregon Trail

Lesson 20 — Canals
- Erie Canal
- Pennsylvania Canal
- Chesapeake & Ohio Canal
- Ohio & Erie Canal
- Miami & Erie Canal

Lesson 21 — North American Territories
- Eastern Woodlands (NE)
- Eastern Woodlands (SE)
- Plains
- Plateau
- Northwest Coast
- California
- Great Basin
- Southwest

Lesson 22 — Deserts
- Mojave Desert
- Sonoran Desert
- Colorado Desert
- Painted Desert
- Great Salt Lake Desert

Lesson 23 — Remarkable Features
- Grand Canyon
- Black Hills
- Ozark Highlands
- Okefenokee Swamp
- Olympic Rainforests
- Niagara Falls

Lesson 24 — Remarkable Features
- Mississippi River Delta
- Mammoth Cave
- San Andreas Fault
- Gulf of Mexico
- Death Valley

117

Lesson 18
Western Rivers
Colorado River
Red River
Rio Grande River
Columbia River
Great Salt Lake

Lesson 19
Historic Trails
Cumberland Road
Santa Fe Trail
Mormon Trail
Gila Trail
Old Spanish Trail
California Trail
Oregon Trail

Lesson 20
Canals
Erie Canal
Pennsylvania Canal
Chesapeake & Ohio
Canal
Ohio & Erie Canal
Miami & Erie Canal

Lesson 21
North American Territories
Eastern Woodlands (NE)
Eastern Woodlands (SE)
Plains
Plateau
Northwest Coast
California
Great Basin
Southwest

Lesson 22
Deserts
Mojave Desert
Sonoran Desert
Colorado Desert
Painted Desert
Great Salt Lake Desert

Lesson 23
Remarkable Features
Grand Canyon
Black Hills
Ozark Highlands
Okefenokee Swamp
Olympic Rainforests
Niagara Falls

Lesson 24
Remarkable Features
Mississippi River Delta
Mammoth Cave
San Andreas Fault
Gulf of Mexico
Death Valley

Blank Summary Map Lessons 18-24

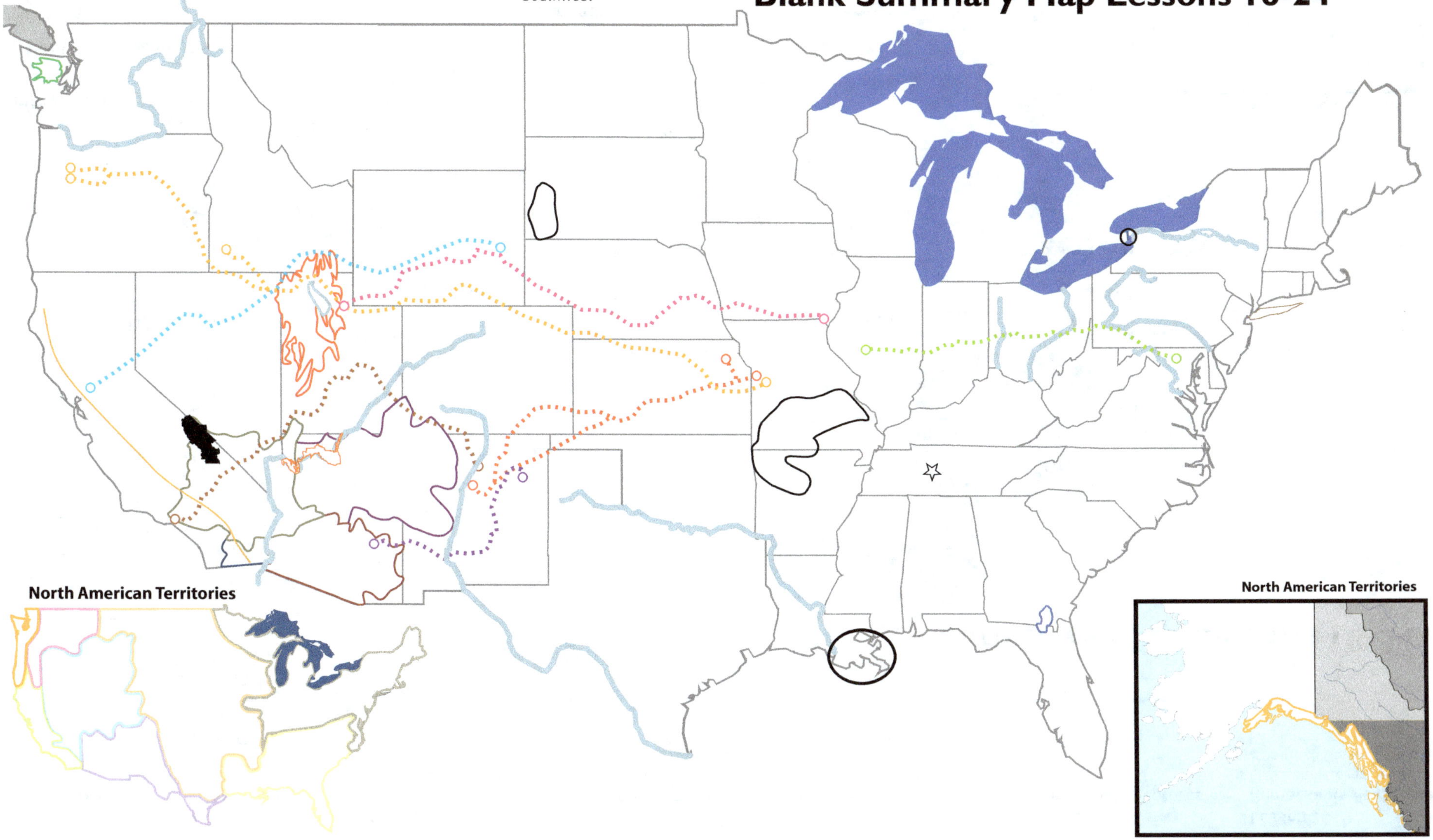

North American Territories

North American Territories

Along the way progression chart

Geography Books

"Ancient Empires & More!"
(Digital Download & Paperback)

"Europe and Asia, Continents, Oceans & More!"
(Digitial Download & Paperback)

"United States & Capitals PLUS Physical Features" 2 BOOKS *(that work together)*:
Teaching & Student Resource Guide*
Includes the Tid-Bits and Master Maps"
(Digitial Download & Paperback)
Student Map Worksheet Book that includes TrueReview*
(Digitial Download & Paperback)
*Digital and Paperback can be bundled or sold separately.

Be sure to check out all resources that compliment the "Where in the World?" Geography Series

Review Games & More

Musical Hop Scotch Mat

Enlarged Map Sets,
Black Line Maps, along with 2 Review Games for these books:

"Ancient Empires & More!"

"Europe and Asia, Continents, Oceans & More!"

"United States & Capitals PLUS Physical Features"

http://bit.ly/WhereInTheWorldGeo